Biblical

Archaeology

Biblical

Archaeology

Allan A. MacRae

Sovereign Grace Publishers, Inc.
P.O. Box 4998
Lafayette, IN 47903
2007

ISBN 1-58960-368-0

*Printed In the United States of America
By Lightning Source, Inc.*

BIBLICAL ARCHAEOLOGY

A. New Vistas for Old Testament Studies

During the first third of the 19th century, as during the two thousand years that preceded, the OT stood practically alone in most of its historical statements.

I. Introduction

All that was known about ancient history at that time went back to about 500 B.C. Before that there were a few statements in some of the Greek writers, but these were so mixed with myths and legends and with miraculous interventions of the pagan gods that they were not considered reliable as sources of historical knowledge. The OT was unique in that it told of events during a period of well over a thousand years preceding 500 B.C. It referred to great cities whose location was no longer known. It mentioned world conquerors whose very names had disappeared. Even whole nations that bulked large in its pages had been completely forgotten. The historical statements of the OT stood alone for the most part. Under these circumstances it was easy for individuals who did not wish to accept the moral and religious teachings of the Bible to question whether its historical statements were dependable. This produced a situation in which students of the higher criticism of the OT felt free to rearrange its sections in such a way as to show a merely natural development of moral and ethical ideas, since many of them were of the opinion that its factual statements were largely mythical and not dependable from a historical viewpoint.

It is no longer possible to take such an approach to the OT. During the past century and a quarter archaeology has repeatedly demonstrated the existence of cities, conquerors, and nations mentioned in the OT. At point after point the background of the OT has been shown to be remarkably accurate. As a result of archaeological investigation and excavation, a whole new world has risen from the dust, so that today history extends just as far back of 500 B.C. as it has proceeded on this side of that date. It can never go still further back, because history is an account of events that is based upon written records, and writing did not come into existence until approximately 3000 B.C. Whatever precedes that time is not history but prehistory.

Biblical archaeology is of importance in relation to NT study, but not nearly as much as in relation to the OT The reasons for this will be discussed in sections VI and VII.

B. Archaeology Defined

Archaeology is not so much a science or a division of knowledge as it is a way of securing knowledge. It is a method for increasing our knowledge of the history of political and social events of past times. Until the rise of archaeology, our knowledge in these areas was based upon material that had been written down and passed on from generation to generation in manuscripts. As old manuscripts wore out, they were copied. The old ones disintegrated; the new ones were in turn copied, and in turn these disintegrated. Thus the Bible and what remains of the classical literature of Greece and Rome were passed on from century to century. These were our only sources for knowledge of ancient times until men began to copy inscriptions on old monuments and to dig in search of buried cities.

Archaeology consists of the examination of materials that were used in ancient times. It is divisible into two parts: first, the study of the remains of ancient buildings, monuments, dishes, statues, and other manifestations of the culture of a given period; second, the study of writings on monuments or in ancient letters, accounts of lawsuits, or other materials of which we have the original copies as written down in ancient times and rediscovered in modern days.

Archaeology is usually restricted to remains of *human* activity in the past. Prehistoric bones, for instance, are considered a part of paleontology rather than of archaeology, unless they are found in connection with objects that would throw light upon the activities of the human beings involved.

C. Biblical Archaeology

Biblical Archaeology is that portion of archaeology which throws light on events or situations described in the Bible. Much of archaeology has no relation to the Bible, but one cannot properly study Biblical archaeology without learning a fair amount about other phases of the subject. Archaeology may deal with any part of the earth in which men have lived, and archaeological discoveries have been made on every continent. Biblical archaeology is principally restricted to the region around the E end of the Mediterranean, and to Mesopotamia, with a little reference to Persia. Even in these regions much of the material

comes from periods when they had no relationships with events recorded in the Bible.

Up to the present, archaeologists have discovered comparatively little material that relates directly and immediately to Biblical statements. There is far more that is indirectly related to them, and there is a vast amount that throws important light upon the general background of the Biblical history.

D. Why Archaeology Is Important ·To the Bible Student

There are four reasons why archaeology is important to the Bible student. The first of these we may designate as general corroboration. Much of the background of the Bible is so different from the historical and cultural situation of our day that it is sometimes easy to imagine that it consists merely of a work of mythology or of imagination. Against this, archaeology presents us with evidence of the existence of the situation that forms the background of the events described in the Bible and thus gives us a general assurance of the reality of the Biblical world. This is one of the most important values of archaeology to the Bible student.

A second great importance of Biblical archaeology might be designated as special corroboration. This deals with points at which archaeological evidence clearly indicates the accuracy of particular statements in the Bible. Many a Biblical statement which had previously been considered to be erroneous or even impossible has thus been shown to be precisely in accord with historic fact.

A third reason, perhaps the most important of all, is the help that archaeology gives for Biblical interpretation. Biblical statements often deal with a specific situation in the past. Archaeology helps us to understand that situation better. Many Biblical words indicate material objects used in Biblical times. Sometimes these objects were very different from those used today. Archaeology enables us to see similar objects and to know more detail about them than could be gained from the Bible. Frequently archaeology makes particular statements in the Bible easier to understand.

A fourth reason archaeology is of interest to the Bible student deals with a new factor that has arisen in recent decades. This might be entitled, "Help in the Study of Derivation." After archaeology began to shed light upon the historical accuracy and dependability of the Bible, some of the enemies of Biblical teaching changed their approach. Admitting its general historical accuracy, they began to allege that its religious and cultural teachings were not original with the Biblical writers but were simply taken over from ideas or attitudes of heathenism. This constitutes a dangerous attack upon Christianity. In some cases it has been carried to a very great extreme. One writer has said that the one whom we worship in our churches is simply an old Babylonian demi-god, named Gilgamesh. Another has said that most of our Christian ideas about Christ are really taken over from aspects of Egyptian religion. Such statements were easy to make when comparatively little was known about the religion and culture of these lands. Now that archaeology has made available tremendous amounts of material on these subjects, it is possible to examine such allegations specifically and exactly, and to see just how much real evidence there is for or against them. This is extremely vital for the defense of Biblical testimony. It opens up a tremendous field of inquiry and is a very important reason for the interest of Bible students in archaeology.

A. The Land of Egypt

We shall begin our examination of Biblical archaeology with Egypt rather than with Palestine. This is not only because extensive materials from Egypt and Mesopotamia were discovered before any great progress in Palestinian archaeology had been made, but also because far more written material has been discovered in these lands than in Palestine. Palestinian archaeology would have been relatively unrewarding if it were not for the many relationships with the work that had already been done in these other countries.

II. Egyptian Archaeology

Egypt has been called "the gift of the Nile." It has so little rainfall that it would be a barren desert if it were not for the fact that the Nile River brings fertility to it. Southern or Upper Egypt consists of a long, narrow strip of land beside the Nile. Northern or Lower Egypt consists of the Nile delta, a region about 140 miles in length and about one hundred miles in width, where the Nile divides into a large number of different mouths, thus producing a wider area of extremely great fertility. As a result of Egypt's very dry climate, archaeological remains have lasted better in Egypt than almost anywhere else in the world. Its colossal ruins form a great outdoor museum. Roman tourists visited the pyramids and other great monuments of Egypt and pondered over their meaning. During the Middle Ages the land was regarded as an area of mystery and enchantment. Naturally it was one of the first regions where archaeology made great advances.

Another feature that is important in the history of Egypt is its isolation. The wilderness protected it on both sides. To the S lay a barren desert, broken only by the course of the Nile.

To the N was the Mediterranean Sea. Only from the NE was it vulnerable, and the few successful attacks in its history usually came from that direction. The very great fertility provided by the constant waters of the Nile and by their annual overflow provided a high level of prosperity which could support a great civilization, while the comparative isolation of the land made possible a long and continuous development of civilization, such as is hard to parallel elsewhere.

B. Egyptian Remains

The ancient kings of Egypt erected enormous monuments to retain their memory, including many statues, obelisks, and temples. Careful and systematic examination of these monuments began in 1798, when Napoleon took a large group of French scientists to Egypt and set them to work to prepare a description of the wonders of Egypt, which was later published. Since that time many scholars have devoted themselves to copying, drawing (and, more recently, to photographing) the ruins of ancient Egypt and to copying its inscriptions, and many sumptuous volumes have been issued. Far less excavation has been done in Egypt than in Mesopotamia or Palestine. One reason is the great amount of knowledge that could be gained in Egypt simply by studying the remains that already stood above the ground.

The pyramids, which are the most imposing remains of ancient Egypt, were a natural development from an earlier form of tomb. About 2700 B.C. a king named Djoser built a tomb composed of five large quadrangular stone houses, one on top of the other, with the size of the upper ones becoming progressively smaller and the whole reaching a height of 190 feet. From this so-called "step pyramid" it was an easy step to a real pyramid. There are many pyramids in Egypt, and the largest of them was the first to be built, by order of King Khufu (often called Cheops). Khufu's intention, like that of Djoser, was to build a burial place for himself, which would also be a memorial of his greatness. He lived much longer than he had expected and therefore from time to time revised the plan of his pyramid, enlarging it greatly, and altering the location of the burial chamber. The resulting monument covers 13 acres and is almost 500 feet in height. It was made of 2,300,000 blocks of limestone, each weighing about 2½ tons. The second pyramid was almost as tall as the first, but somewhat narrower at the bottom, and therefore steeper. All of the pyramids were broken into in ancient times, and the bodies of the pharaohs were removed, along with many precious objects that had been buried with them. A few of the pyramids contain texts written on the walls of their inner passages and chambers. These "Pyramid Texts" are a description of the glorious future which awaits the pharaoh in his afterlife as he makes his entrance among the gods. The Pyramid Texts tell much about Egyptian beliefs regarding the next world, but very little about earthly life in ancient Egypt.

The Great Pyramid was a burial place and memorial for Khufu, and nothing else. Assertions that it in some way indicates the prophetic history of the world or tells anything about the Christian religion are entirely imaginary. There is no basis for such claims either in the Bible or in any ancient Egyptian writing.

Mention should also be made of the material objects and pictures found in the tombs of the nobles. Many of these are beautifully colored and portray ordinary life on the large estates of the nobles. They have proven a great source for understanding the life and culture of the ancient Egyptians.

The monuments and other objects remaining from ancient Egypt are very extensive, but Biblical archaeology has far more contacts with the written material from Egypt than with the physical remains.

C. Egyptian Writing

1. The Decipherment

During the Middle Ages it was generally thought that the pictures of men, women, animals, and plants that decorated many of the monuments of Egypt had a magical purpose. Actually, they represented a strange type of writing, the meaning of which had been completely forgotten. When Napoleon's engineers were preparing defense works near the Rosetta mouth of the Nile in 1798, they came upon a stone which contained a fairly long inscription, written in three different types of writing. At the top were several lines in the hieroglyphic or picture writing which was familiar from its occurrence on the great Egyptian monuments. Below was writing in a different type of character (later called demotic). Still further down was writing in Greek characters, stating that some priests had put up this monument to express their thanks to King Ptolemy V (about 200 B.C.) for remitting certain taxes that they had formerly been required to pay. In 1802 the British captured this part of Egypt, and among the plunder seized from Napoleon's forces was the "Rosetta Stone," which was taken to England and stands today in the British Museum.

Decipherment of the Rosetta Stone proved to be a very difficult problem. Many scholars tried their hand at it, but it was nearly 20 years before success was attained. The Greek version was easy to read and it was a good guess that the other two types of writing gave the same message. However, no one knew anything about the language, or about the type of writing involved. Eventually a young French scholar, named J. F. Champollion, succeeded in comparing proper names in the Greek section with certain signs that occurred at the corresponding places in the hieroglyphic lines. Champollion was a student of Coptic, the language of Egypt in the early Christian centuries. On the assumption that the ancient language was somewhat similar he made guesses as to the pronunciation of some of the words in the hieroglyphic text. In 1822, he published his interpretation of the hieroglyphic writing, and a solid foundation was laid for subsequent study of the language of ancient Egypt.

2. The Nature of the Writing

The hieroglyphic writing was a system different from anything that had ever been discovered before. It had begun as a sort of picture writing, in which an actual picture was to convey the desired message. Eventually, however, certain pictures came to represent particular words. Thus a drawing that depicted a man's legs might simply mean "to run," and could be used after a picture of a man, a woman, or even a cow, to indicate that the one referred to was running. In the Egyptian language, as in Hebrew, and even sometimes in English (cf. *sit* and *sat*, or *write* and *wrote*), words regularly changed their tense or other relationship by changing their vowels while keeping the consonants the same. Hence the hieroglyphic sign came to represent only the consonants involved, and not the vowels. Consequently, the same sign sometimes indicated any one of several words that were entirely unrelated, but happened to have the same consonants. Thus the picture of an eye, which means

5

"to see," is also commonly used to mean "to do," since this word has the same consonants. In time, weak consonants in certain words ceased to be pronounced at all, so that a sign came to represent a succession of two consonants instead of three, or even to represent only one consonant. Since often the same picture could stand for any one of several words, it became customary to put a general picture, called a determinative, before a noun to indicate the class of objects to which it belonged. Then the picture indicating the specific word would be usually followed by another sign to represent a word that contained only its last two consonants, and by still a fourth sign to show its final consonant. These peculiar features of the hieroglyphic writing make it extremely difficult to represent in Latin letters and have resulted in great variety in the forms in which historians have spelled Egyptian proper names in Latin letters. Thus we find the name of the god Amun often written in our histories as Amen or Amon. The "heretic king," Akhenaton (see below), may be referred to, in various books, as Achnaton, Echnaton, Akhnaton, or Ikhnaton. King Thutmose sometimes appears as Tutmosis or Tothmes.

For nearly three thousand years hieroglyphics continued to be written on Egyptian monuments, but for ordinary usage another type of writing became much more common. Papyrus plants were found in great abundance along the Nile, and it was easy to use them to make a sort of paper called papyrus. On this papyrus scribes wrote with ink, and very soon a shortened form of the hieroglyphic writing, called hieratic, became common, in which a group of two or three hieroglyphics would often be represented by a greatly abbreviated line or figure. Great numbers of hieroglyphic inscriptions have been preserved

on the Egyptian monuments, chiseled in stone, and often highly colored, but most of the hieratic writing has disappeared, since the papyrus has disintegrated. However, a number of papyrus documents, some of them quite long, have been preserved as a result of being buried in the dry tombs of Upper Egypt. Hieratic writing often differs strikingly in different hands and as written in different times. The reading of hieratic is largely done by a comparatively few experts who translate it into the hieroglyphic signs that the hieratic represents. Many of the hieratic manuscripts have been published in the form of transliteration into hieroglyphics and thus are available for study even by students of ancient Egyptian who have not devoted a great amount of time to the specific study of hieratic.

In the last few centuries before the time of Christ a still more simplified method of writing developed which is known as the demotic or popular writing. This was commonly used not for religious or state documents, but for accounts and business matters. It is the type of writing in the second group of signs on the Rosetta Stone.

Thus, the Egyptian writing greatly changed its form during the centuries. Yet the hieroglyphics themselves remained substantially the same to the very end of ancient Egyptian history. Eventually they had come to be used mostly as a decorative type of writing, principally on monuments. The Egyptians thought of the hieroglyphics almost as living pictures rather than merely as written symbols. Thus the picture of a serpent, which represents the sound *f*, is always drawn on the monuments in two parts, with a space in the middle of it, so that it is plain that the serpent is dead and cannot hurt anyone.

After Alexander's conquest (332 B.C.), which began the Hellenistic age in Egypt, many features of Greek culture were incorporated into Egyptian life. Eventually, people began to use a modified Greek alphabet to represent the Egyptian language as it was then spoken. This writing is called Coptic. Its signs have no relation to those used in ancient Egypt, but the language itself is a direct descendant of the language used on the earliest monuments. Since Greek writing, unlike the earlier systems, expresses vowels, the Coptic has been an invaluable tool for the study of the Egyptian language, and has thrown much light on its vocalization.

3. The Egyptian Language

After Champollion opened the door to the reading of the hieroglyphics, many scholars studied the material and eventually grammars were written for the language as used at various periods. Such German scholars as Erman and Sethe carried this investigation to a very high degree of accuracy. While the absence of vowels inevitably results in a certain amount of indefiniteness, ancient Egyptian historical inscriptions can now be translated without much question as to their meaning. Other writings, such as the Pyramid Texts and the Book of the Dead, occasionally contain passages which would be difficult to render accurately regardless of the language used. With help from John D. Rockefeller, Jr., the University of Berlin has issued a very extensive dictionary of ancient Egyptian.

4. Egyptian Literature

From the viewpoint of a student of history, Egyptian literature is at first sight rather disappointing. There are no historical writings similar to the book of Genesis or the books of Samuel and Kings. No attempt is made to give a full picture of a historical situation or development. A continuous account of

the reign of successive kings has nowhere been found, though it is true that many kings put up monuments to celebrate particular victories or outstanding events, and these give a considerable amount of historical information. A great handicap in the study of Egyptian literature, as far as its use for history is concerned, is the fact that most of it was written for an immediate purpose, often merely to glorify the person involved, and never simply to preserve historical truth. Tombs of the nobles sometimes contain statements about the great deeds they had performed, and these throw incidental light upon many details of history. Our fullest historical sources are a few rather lengthy accounts of the military affairs of a king's reign, written on papyrus and buried with him, in order to show how much booty he had given to the gods, and thus to secure a reward for him in the afterlife or a blessing upon his posterity. Some of these give rather full accounts of an extended series of military campaigns; yet they leave us with the feeling that they are abbreviated from more extensive annals that have completely perished. Some Egyptian papyri contain what might be designated as "fine writing," since it was greatly treasured for its style. These generally consist of stories of incidents that were not particularly important in themselves; yet from them considerable light is sometimes thrown upon history. Egyptian literature tells much about the cultural life, religion, and general outlook of the ancient Egyptians, but its interpretation in precise historical terms is sometimes rather baffling.

D. The History of Ancient Egypt

1. Chronology

The ancient Egyptians did not have any system of numbering years continuously for longer than a single reign. Usually a year w is indicated according to its position in the reign of a pharaoh, and a new numbering began with the next pharaoh. Taking the highest numbers used in each of them, it was possible to construct a rough chronology, and further study of the great number of writings that we possess has made it possible to enlarge this very considerably. Synchronisms with events in other countries have sometimes been available. An invaluable aid has been the so-called Sothic cycle, or phoenix year. This is based upon the fact that at a very early time the Egyptians adopted a calendar of 365 days. Since this is approximately a fourth of a day shorter than the actual time that it takes the earth to go around the sun, the years became one day off every four years, so that after a few hundred years a date that had previously been in midsummer would come in midwinter. In about 1460 years the calendar would go completely around the cycle and again begin at the same time of year. Eventually it came to be thought that the day on which the star Sirius (also called Sothis), the brightest star in the heavens, rises just before sunrise should be the first day in the year. Sometimes at periods several hundred years apart we find a statement that this day which should be the first of the year actually occurred at another specified date, thus showing how many days off the calendar was at that time. This gives us a means of telling within four years the date within a cycle when a particular document was written, but does not tell in which cycle it was. It used to be thought that there were a number of cycles between certain of the great events in Egyptian history. Now it is pretty well agreed that this is not the case, and the so-called long chronology is hardly held any more. Many of the dates in early Egyptian his-

tory can be agreed upon with considerable certainty by Egyptologists, but never closer than within four years, and sometimes there is considerable diversity of opinion.

It is interesting that as recently as 1930, J. H. Breasted, one of our greatest authorities on ancient Egyptian history, insisted that 4241 B.C. was the date when the Egyptians established their calendar. It is doubtful if today any recognized Egyptologist would place this event as early as 3000 B.C.

It is usual to think of ancient Egyptian history as divided into 30 dynasties. This idea is taken from a book on *Egyptian History* by Manetho, an Egyptian priest, who wrote at about 250 B.C. Selections from Manetho's book have been preserved in extensive quotations by later writers. Manetho was able to read the names of the Egyptian kings on the monuments, and seems to have arranged them into the 30 groups, which he called dynasties. The division is sometimes rather arbitrary, but has proven quite convenient. The names of the kings, which Manetho wrote in Greek, were considerably changed in the course of transmission.

2. Prehistory

The time before writing began is called prehistory. In Egypt this period is evidenced by a number of remains, but has little connection with any Biblical statements. It is quite certain that many sections of Egypt became united under local rulers, and eventually these coalesced into two main sections called Upper and Lower Egypt. Eventually, these two were united under the first dynasty, but to the very end of ancient Egyptian history the kings were styled "King of Upper and Lower Egypt," and often represented with two different crowns, one for each section.

3. The Old Kingdom

Egyptian history begins with the invention of writing, about the time of the first dynasty. The hieroglyphic system is soon quite fully developed, so it would seem likely that its impetus came from knowledge of a written system (called cuneiform) which had had a longer and slower development in Mesopotamia. The Egyptian system developed along very different lines from those in Mesopotamia.

The Old Kingdom is the title given to the first time of great royal power (about 2700 to 2200 B.C.), running from dynasties three to six. At this period the pharaohs were very dictatorial. They were able to gather hundreds of thousands of people each year during the season when the Nile overflowed its banks and made agricultural work impossible and compel them to work energetically for long periods in order to build those tremendous burial monuments called the pyramids. During this time the religion glorified the sun god, but there were many subordinate deities. Eventually the power of the pharaoh crumbled and there was a time of disorganization, during the latter part of which some of the great classics of Egyptian literature were written.

4. The Middle Kingdom

A new time of great power began when the kings of a region in the S, centering around the town later known as Thebes, and worshiping a local god called Amun (formerly written Amen or Amon), became supreme over all of Egypt and established their power in the delta. This was the period of the Twelfth Dynasty (about 1991 to 1786 B.C.). These kings put foreign lands under tribute, and directed a high type of civilization, though without quite the same monarchical supremacy as that of either the Old Kingdom or the later

New Kingdom. This is the classical time of Egyptian literature. It ends with the coming from Asia of a foreign group that possessed a new weapon, that of horse-drawn chariots which enabled them to make a lightning attack and to conquer a large section of Egypt. These Hyksos (sometimes called Shepherd-kings), held much of the land in subjection for over a century. Eventually they were driven out. Instead of putting up monuments to celebrate their deliverance, the Egyptians preferred to forget that they had ever been under foreign control. Details of the Hyksos invasion are known to us principally from later incidental references, and also from statements in the tombs of some of the nobles about the part they themselves had played in the driving out of the Hyksos.

5. The Empire

The period of the New Kingdom, also called the Empire, followed the expulsion of the Hyksos. This period begins at about 1570 B.C., with the 18th dynasty. These kings, like those of the Middle Kingdom, worshiped the god Amun, whom they considered to be identical with the earlier sun-god, Re, and therefore often referred to as Amun-Re. A multitude of other gods were also worshiped in Egypt, but the priests of Amun-Re became so important that eventually a very large proportion of the land of Egypt came to be the property of the temples of the god Amun. The 18th dynasty includes a series of great rulers, a number of whom went by one of the two names: Thutmose or Amenhotep. This was a time of Egyptian military prowess, and of the erection of great monuments and temples. The history of religion finds special interest in the so-called heretic king, Akhenaton (also called Amenhotep IV), who reigned from about 1370 to 1353 B.C. In sharp contrast with his predecessors, he was a real monotheist, worshiping only the material disk of the sun. He tried to do away with the ancient Egyptian polytheism and desired to build a new capital city where only Aton should ever have been worshiped. Therefore he moved his capital to a new place, later called El Amarna. While preoccupied with religious and philosophical matters, he allowed the Egyptian empire that Thutmose III and others had developed to fall into decay. His successors moved the capital back to Thebes, abandoning the new capital city, which had been occupied only a few years. Modern excavators have found at El Amarna the remains of the buildings that characterized the Egyptian capital in the reign of Akhenaton. This is the place where, in 1887, the famous Tell el-Amarna letters were found, consisting of about three hundred clay tablets written in the cuneiform writing of Mesopotamia, but containing messages between Akhenaton or his father and the kings of Canaan or the rulers of other sections of the ancient world. These letters are of great value for reconstructing the history of that period. After Akhenaton had died, and the triumph of the priests of Amun had resulted in the capital's being moved back to Thebes, Akhenaton was always referred to as a malefactor. The general confusion that now occurred put an end to the 18th dynasty.

The 19th dynasty (about 1303 to 1197), even more than the 18th, was a period of great building. Largely as a result of the activities of the kings of these two dynasties, tremendous ruins stand at Thebes today, making it the great outdoor museum of the world. Ramses II reigned for 67 years (about 1290 to 1224) and left many records of his great military exploits. Yet he outlived his energy and his son Mer-

neptah (about 1224 to 1214) became king when already an old man. His monuments claim that he repeated the exploits of his father, but his boasting statements are greatly discounted by historians.

Ramses III (about 1195 to 1164), the second king of the 20th dynasty, drove back a great invasion of sea peoples which attacked Egypt by sea and land. One of these peoples is considered to have been the Philistines. Driven away from Egypt, they settled on the S part of the coastland of Palestine. Ramses III was succeeded by a series of monarchs of declining power, also bearing the name of Ramses. During the Empire Period there had been many great expeditions into Palestine, Syria, and other countries, and tremendous amounts of plunder had been brought to Egypt to increase the glory of the pharaoh and to enrich the temples of Amun.

During the next five hundred years lesser rulers struggled to maintain the glories of Egypt but fell far short of the achievements of their predecessors.

6. The Persian Period

After a brief time of being in subjection to the Assyrians or to the Babylonians, Egypt came into the hands of the Persian rulers of the ancient world (525-332). During this time there was a Jewish military colony in Elephantine, far S in Egypt. This colony left important records in the Aramaic language, known as the Elephantine papyri, which shed considerable light upon the period of the exile.

7. The Hellenistic Period

In 332 B.C. Alexander the Great conquered Egypt. After his death in 323, one of his generals, named Ptolemy, seized Egypt and established a dynasty that continued for three centuries. These rulers brought Greek blood into the control of Egypt but maintained the fiction of continuing the organization and trappings of the pharaohs.

8. The Roman Period

After the conquest of Cleopatra by Octavian in 30 B.C., Egypt was incorporated into the Roman Empire. Large numbers of Jews lived in Alexandria, which was a great center of Hellenistic culture. The land continued under Roman power until the Arabic conquest in A.D. 641, which destroyed many of the remains of the life and culture of ancient Egypt. Desiring to build a new capital in which no heathen god would have been worshiped, the Arabs established the city of Cairo just S of the delta, and took many of the remains of the great capital city called Memphis, which was only ten miles away, to use as building stones for Cairo.

E. Relation of Egyptian Archaeology to the Bible

1. General Corroboration

In the area of general corroboration, Egyptian archaeology has great interest for the Bible student. In the early part of the Bible, Egypt appears as the outstanding power of the day. This is the land to which the Israelites go for help in time of famine. Here the posterity of Jacob increases until it becomes a great nation. God's marvelous power is displayed in rescuing the Israelites from Egyptian oppression. Toward the end of the OT history there is a vital change. Israelite kings still tend to look to Egypt as a counterforce to protect them from Assyrian or Babylonian attack, but the prophets warn them against putting trust in Egypt (cf. Isa. 30:1-7).

All these features of the general background of the Biblical narrative are abundantly illustrated by material from Egypt.

It is a mistake to think of the Israelites as having any part in the building of the pyramids. This occurred at least a thousand years before the time of Joseph. The first Biblical contact with Egypt is when Abram goes there for help in time of famine. Such visits of Asiatics to Egypt are illustrated by a picture in an Egyptian tomb from this general period, showing a picturesque group of 37 Asiatics visiting Egypt. Another such picture shows Syrian cattle in Egypt, addressed by a herdsman who says: "Once you trod the sand, now you walk on herbage."

The background of the story of Joseph contains many passages that can be vividly illustrated by Egyptian circumstance at this general period. Thus we find in Egyptian records that the position that Potiphar gave Joseph when he put him over his household was one that existed in the houses of great Egyptian nobles of the time; that the king of Egypt was called "pharaoh," the term used in the Bible; that "chief of the butlers" and "chief of the bakers" were titles given to important officers in pharaoh's court; that the signet ring, the "vestures of fine linen," and the "gold chain about his neck" were just what an Egyptian king would be apt to give to one whom he was placing in authority over the whole country; and that the mummification of Jacob and of Joseph was in accordance with Egyptian custom. These and other elements of the general background can be abundantly verified from ancient Egyptian records. All this is general corroboration. Special corroboration would mean the finding of the particular name of Joseph or of some specific act that he performed. Instances of special corroboration from this early period are extremely few.

Exodus pictures Egypt not only as a

fertile and prosperous nation but also as a land of great cruelty. Egyptian monuments show the pharaoh (pictured large), holding several men in his hand and dashing them to pieces, or shooting his arrows into great multitudes of enemies. One Egyptian king had a doorstep fashioned to look like the prostrate figure of a certain Asiatic king, so that every time he entered or left his palace he stepped on the back of the figure of his enemy. Egyptian remains from this period vividly illustrate the Biblical picture of cruelty and oppression.

During the latter part of Israelite history Egyptian power was much weaker than at earlier periods. Eventually, Mesopotamian armies overran Egypt, proving the correctness of the prophetic warnings.

Egyptian material is of great value for general corroboration. It is disappointing to find that the amount of it available for special corroboration is far less than might be expected.

2. Special Corroboration

Two very interesting cases of special corroboration are involved in Genesis 12:16, where Abraham is described as having acquired considerable property in Egypt and a catalog of his wealth is given. In this list there is no mention of horses. In later times Egypt was the great land of the horse, and it would be difficult for anyone who invented a story like this in the time of the later Israelite kingdom to fail to mention horses in the list of the property that Abraham amassed. It is only in comparatively recent years that examination of Egyptian antiquity has led to the discovery that the horse was unknown in Egypt until the time of the Hyksos invasion. It was by the use of horse-drawn chariots that the Hyksos made their successful "lightning attacks" on the land of Egypt. After the Hyksos were driven out, the Egyptians saw to it that they were always well equipped with horses, and Egypt became widely known as the land of the best horses (cf. I Kings 10:28-29).

The mention of camels at the end of Genesis 12:16 formerly produced a very important problem in special corroboration. Thus in the 1930 edition of the *Encyclopedia Britannica*, H. R. Hall, Director of Antiquities in the British Museum, made the statement that the camel was unknown in Egypt until the late Persian period, or approximately the fourth century B.C. This would contradict the Biblical statement that more than a thousand years earlier Abraham had amassed a great number of camels in Egypt. For some reason the nobles did not care to have camels pictured on the paintings in their tombs, and the camel is seldom mentioned in Egyptian references. Yet a rope of camel hair has now been discovered from a time as early as the middle of the second millennium B.C. Other scanty and yet very definite evidence from figurines and other sources makes it clear that the camel was indeed present in Egypt at the time of Abraham, even though at first sight this looked like a real problem in the Biblical narrative.

From a much later period, we find king Shishak boasting of his conquests in Palestine, which are mentioned in I Kings 14:25-28 and in II Chronicles 12:2-9. Not only the event, but also the Egyptian name, Sheshonk, which would be represented in Hebrew writing as Shishak, is an interesting specific corroboration of the accuracy of the Biblical narrative.

The same is true of the reference in II Kings 19:9, and in the parallel in Isa. 37:9, to "Tirhakah, King of Ethiopia" as coming out to fight the king of Assyria. It is now known that a dynasty of Ethiopian kings ruled over Egypt at this time. One of these kings, named Tirhakah, is mentioned in cuneiform inscriptions as a formidable opponent of the Assyrians.

There are a few other valuable instances of special corroboration from Egypt. We must, however, give consideration to the question, why material of this type is not more extensive.

3. Why Not More Egyptian Material For Special Corroboration

In view of the great amount of archaeological material that has been preserved in ancient Egypt, the thousands of inscriptions, the many interesting pictures and statues, and the great number of books that have been written describing various features of the culture and the history of ancient Egypt, it is disappointing to find comparatively few relationships between it and the Bible. While there are points at which Egyptian archaeology is of real importance for the Scriptures, these are far fewer than one would expect, or than one finds, for instance, in Mesopotamia. The Bible student should know the reasons for this situation. The first of these is the fact that the Egyptian material is so largely made up of monuments or other material prepared in order to glorify someone. These monuments do not give us a full-orbed picture of Egyptian life, but only present what the noble or the king desires to be remembered. In Mesopotamia we have a far more rounded picture of the total life of the nation.

A second reason is the fact that in their relationship with Israel the Egyptians had comparatively little of which to boast. One of the outstanding incidents in the Bible is the mighty deliverance of the Israelites from Egypt by the outstretched hand of God, but we would

hardly expect the Egyptians to celebrate such a defeat. In a school history of the United States the account of the War of 1812 is apt to tell a good bit about the victory of isolated American ships over British ships, but the disastrous attempt to conquer Canada may be passed over with a word or two. On the contrary, the Canadian school history is apt to say little or nothing about the American sea victories but to speak in glowing terms about the gallant Canadian forces that utterly defeated the attempts of the Yankees to conquer Canada. Every nation likes to celebrate the things in which it can find reason to boast. Lack of Egyptian material bearing directly on the Exodus of the Israelites might raise some question as to the accuracy of the Biblical account, if it were not for the nature of the Egyptian remains and for the fact that there was in this event nothing of which they could boast. It is quite different when we come to a far less important Biblical incident, that of Shishak's invasion of Palestine. This occupies only a few lines in the Biblical acount, but in Egypt Shishak put up a great inscription on a temple wall to celebrate his Palestinian expedition, and named at length the cities that he claimed to have conquered.

Still another factor should be mentioned. A very great part of the stirring events of ancient Egyptian history took place in the delta, the most prosperous section of the land, and also the one nearest to Asia and consequently most involved in the frequent preparations for warlike expeditions into Asia and most in danger of attack from that region. The great majority of the relationships between the Bible and Egypt doubtless took place in the delta region, yet perhaps nine-tenths of our remains from Egypt come from Upper Egypt and comparatively little from the delta. The reason for this is that the delta has continued as a center of active life all through history and the remains of ancient times are covered by the teeming population of today. In addition, the water level in the delta has been constantly rising, so that even if it were possible to remove houses, factories, and farms, so as to excavate in the delta, one would not go very deep before the material would be all covered with water, subject to much corruption and decay, and extremely difficult to excavate or to study. On the other hand, in Upper Egypt where a thin line of occupation runs beside the Nile, behind which one need go only a short distance to reach complete wilderness, there is a little-disturbed region for erection of great monuments and for making burials. Thus, S Egypt is to quite an extent a great outdoor museum, but a tremendous portion of it contains what its people desired to celebrate, rather than the incidental remains of their human life and activity.

4. Interpretation

Egyptian records are not as helpful in Biblical interpretation as those from Mesopotamia, but there are a number of places at which Biblical words or situations can be better understood in view of the light from ancient Egypt. One of these to which allusion has been made above is its striking illustration of the reality and extent of the oppression to which the Israelites were subjected in the period just before the Exodus. Another interesting instance is the use of the word *hanikim* in Genesis 14:14 (translated "trained" in the A.V.). This word, which describes the men whom Abraham led out to fight, occurs nowhere else in the OT. It is used in Egyptian records from this time as a designation for the armed retainers of Palestinian chieftans.

5. Particular Problems

In view of the great gaps in our knowledge of particular points at which Egyptian history and Biblical history touch, it is not surprising that there should be a number of very interesting problems, some of which can now be solved, while others cannot. Two of these will be mentioned here. (1) One is the rather puzzling story about the bricks and the straw in Exodus 5:14-19. As a result of unexpected developments, this problem can now be quite satisfactorily explained. For its elucidation see the article *Bricks without Straw*. (2) A second problem, which, however, is still far from solved, is the date of the Exodus. In Genesis and Exodus the Egyptian kings are referred to only by the title "pharaoh" and the personal name is never given. The Egyptian kings found nothing to boast of in the Exodus and put up no monuments to celebrate it. Some have questioned whether it actually occurred, though most scholars are ready to admit that a nation would never imagine slavery in another country as having been at the beginning of its national history, unless this had actually occurred. The absence of specific Egyptian evidence of the Exodus makes it difficult to know just where to fit it in among the various kings of Egypt, and various theories have been advanced. Some Bible scholars would base everything upon one particular interpretation of one verse of Scripture (1 Kings 6:1). While this interpretation may be true, yet there are other ways of interpreting the verse, and since it stands alone the possibility must be recognized that it might involve an error of transmission of text. The evidence is at present far from clear as to the time of the Exodus, and consequently it seems the wise policy for the Bible student, while awaiting further archaeological evidence, to admit that we do not know just when it occurred. However, we insist that it did occur, exactly as described in the Bible. (Cf. also the remarks in section V.E.6.)

6. The Problem of Derivation

It is sometimes asserted that Egyptian evidence explains the origin of many of the religious and cultural ideas in the Bible. Most of the instances where Hebrew religious ideas are said to have been borrowed from Egypt are rather farfetched and disappear upon close examination, but there are a few cases that require detailed investigation. We shall mention two of these:

(1) Joseph and Potiphar's wife. A papyrus manuscript that was written about 1225 B.C., in the 19th dynasty, contains an Egyptian folktale about two brothers. It begins with a situation involving the younger brother and the wife of the older brother that is strikingly similar to the experience of Joseph with Potiphar's wife, described in Gen. 39. Barton says: "Scholars of the critical school regard this as the original of the story in Genesis (G. A. Barton, *Archaeology and the Bible*, 7th ed., 1937, p. 367). However, this is not the most likely interpretation of the relationship between the two stories. The Egyptian *Story of the Two Brothers* is a very bizarre and fantastic tale, utterly unlike the matter-of-fact account of Joseph's experience. Thus when the older brother tries to ambush the younger brother who has been falsely accused by the older brother's wife, the oxen tell the younger brother that the older brother is hiding behind the door in order to kill him. The younger brother flees for his life, and the older brother pursues him, with his lance in his hand. The younger brother cries out to the sun god for help, and the sun god causes a body of water to spring up between the two brothers, full of crocodiles, so that the older brother cannot reach the younger brother, who now has a chance to declare his innocence. After the older brother returns home, the younger brother puts his own heart on the flower of a cedar tree for safekeeping. The gods fashion a beautiful wife for him, but she eventually leaves him in order to live with the king of Egypt. At her suggestion the pharaoh sends men to cut down the cedar tree, which immediately causes the younger brother to die. The older brother has by this time become convinced of his younger brother's innocence and has therefore killed his own wife and thrown her to the dogs. One day he finds his liquor tasting bad and learns from this that his younger brother needs him; so he goes to the fallen cedar tree to look for his brother's heart. After a three-year search he finds it and soaks it in cold water, which he gives his brother to drink. This brings him back to life. The younger brother then assumes the form of a bull, and his brother takes him to the court. He reveals himself to his wife but she induces the pharaoh to sacrifice the bull. Two drops of his blood fall to the ground and cause two great trees to grow up. The wife asks pharaoh to have the trees chopped down. A splinter flies off and enters the mouth of the wife, who soon bears a son, which is another rebirth of the husband. Eventually he becomes king and makes his older brother prime minister.

Most discussions of the theory that this is the source of the story of Joseph and Potiphar's wife only quote the first third of it. Although this first part contains certain magical elements, they are far less numerous and less grotesque than those in the rest of the story. Rather than to think that the incident in the life of Joseph was modeled upon this grotesque folktale, which is definitely later than the time of Joseph, it is more reasonable to think that the relation is just the reverse. The story of how Joseph rose from being an imprisoned slave to become the leader of the Egyptian government must have been widely discussed, and every known incident of his life repeated over and over in all sections of Egypt. His experience with Potiphar's wife could easily have become the foundation of a folk story, to which all sorts of bizarre and fantastic elements were added as it passed from mouth to mouth. The existence of a story of this type in Egypt from a period considerably later than the time of Joseph is an evidence of the truth of the story of Joseph rather than a proof that this grotesque story was a source from which the incident might have passed into the Bible. When the *Tale of the Two Brothers* in its entirety, with all its extravagances and fanciful elements, is compared with the simply told and natural story of Joseph and Potiphar's wife, it is easy to see which is the derived story and which is the original.

(2) It has been claimed that the incident of the so-called heretic king, to which allusion has been made above (II.D.5), was the real source of Hebrew monotheism. One of the last books written by the late Sigmund Freud was entitled *Moses and Monotheism*. In this book he asserted that Moses was an Egyptian nobleman who took over the lofty teaching of the pharaoh Akhenaton and taught it to a group of Hebrew slaves whom he subsequently led out of Egypt. However, Freud faces a problem in that the liberal critics maintain that the Hebrews were not monotheists until many centuries after the time of the Exodus. He gets around this by alleging that the Israelites killed Moses in the wilderness and that this event produced a trauma in their

subconscious, with the result that the monotheistic ideas that they had learned from Moses became buried in their subconscious and were passed on from father to son, until in the time of Amos this monotheism came to expression in the teaching of the great writing prophets.

It is to be feared that Freud's theory here reaches one of the lowest points ever attained by Biblical criticism or by psychoanalytic theory. In addition, investigation of the teaching of Akhenaton has brought out two very important differences between his beliefs and those of the OT: (1) while the teaching of Akhenaton is actually monotheistic and hence unique in ancient Egypt, its monotheism consists in the belief in the material disk of the sun as the sole god; (2) the religion of Akhenaton is entirely lacking in ethical elements and consequently utterly different from the ethical monotheism which finds such superb expression in the writings of Amos, Isaiah, and the other writing prophets. It is much more reasonable to think that Akhenaton, who had close relationship with Asia and with Asiatics, was, either directly or through his mother, affected by a teaching that represented a corruption of the revelation that God had given to the Hebrews, than to believe that Hebrew monotheism was in any way derived from the teaching of Akhenaton.

III. Mesopotamia More materials of importance in relation to the Bible have come from Mesopotamia than from any other area, even including Palestine. Some of the incidents are less dramatic than those involving Egypt, but they are of great importance.

A. The Geographical Background

Mesopotamia, like Egypt, is a region of very great fertility, well adapted for the rise of a great civilization. As the name suggests, it differs from Egypt in being the result not of one river but of two. The Tigris and the Euphrates bring water and fertility to a region that would otherwise be very dry and desolate, though not nearly as dry as Egypt.

This region was not as isolated as Egypt. The wilderness around it was less barren, and contained some tribes who could bring danger to the fertile land. The mountains to the E and N were filled with many tribes, looking down with envy and desire upon the prosperous valley country. Enemies could follow the Euphrates from the W. Invaders could land in the S in boats, and this was probably the source of a great prehistoric conquest. Mesopotamian history constitutes a patchwork of many different forces and seems far more complicated than Egyptian history.

A primary difference between the life of Mesopotamia and that of Egypt is the result of a physical situation. Egypt had great numbers of papyrus plants growing along the Nile, and from them a sort of paper called papyrus was made, which made writing easy and was a tremendous help in the development of Egyptian economic and cultural life. However, these Egyptian papyri have almost entirely disappeared, except for those few that were buried in tombs. Since Mesopotamia had no such easy source of writing material as papyrus, a rather poor substitute was invented, that of making clay tablets, the size of a cake of soap or larger, and writing on these by pressing them with a stylus, so as to make a line that was a little wider at one end than at the other. These clay tablets were much more cumbersome and awkward than the papyrus so readily available in Egypt. However, from our viewpoint they had one great advantage, that of being far more durable. If the clay tablets were

baked, as was sometimes done, they became almost imperishable. Mesopotamian remains include not only the monuments and other records that the leaders wished preserved—and of these we have a great many—but also a tremendous amount of the ephemeral writing of the people. Almost everything written in ancient Mesopotamia eventually came to be buried under the accumulating debris of ongoing civilization. Excavation brings to light not only inscriptions of kings, but also incidental contracts of common people. The cumbersomeness of having to use clay tablets for writing proved to be a great advantage for future generations, in that we can know the ordinary life of the people of Mesopotamia to an extent that was impossible in Egypt. While Mesopotamia lacks the great number of beautiful pictures in the tombs of the Egyptian nobles portraying so many details of common life, we have a far greater number of writings that deal with incidental matters.

B. Excavation in Mesopotamia

1. History of Exploration And Excavation

The cities of Mesopotamia were generally built on terraces made of bricks, and the walls were of the same material. In time, some of the bricks deteriorated and covered the remains of cities that had been abandoned. Even in peace time the cities tended to grow higher since refuse was generally thrown out into the streets. In case of war, a city might be knocked down and left a ruin, and then eventually a new city might be built on top of it. Thus the cities grew higher, but in time most of the remains were so completely buried that as late as the beginning of the 19th century, even the location of most of them was completely unknown.

17

Excavation began in 1842 with the work of a French vice-consul, T. E. Botta. He and others excavated in and around the site of Nineveh, the capital of the ancient Assyrian Empire, in the N portion of Mesopotamia. Consequently, the science of study of ancient Mesopotamia came to be called Assyriology, and this name was used for the entire subject until the 20th century was well under way. Soon after Botta began his work, a young Englishman, A. H. Layard, began excavation at Nineveh. Layard showed remarkable ability at writing up the results of his work and at highlighting its relation to the Bible. His accounts aroused tremendous interest. Others continued the work of these men until about 1860. By this time a great number of statues and other relics of ancient times had been excavated, and many of them had been taken to the foremost museums of Europe. For about ten years interest in excavation waned. Then it was suddenly reawakened by a rather dramatic event.

In December, 1872, George Smith, an employee of the British Museum, announced that he had found among the tablets brought from Nineveh an account of the Flood which closely resembled that in the Bible. Great interest was aroused by his report and the proprietors of the London Daily Telegraph contributed money to send George Smith to hunt for additional tablets. Smith led two expeditions, extended the trenches of his predecessors at Nineveh and discovered many important inscriptions, but in 1876 he suddenly died of fever at Aleppo. His career had stirred the interest of the whole W world, so that many W nations then began excavations in Mesopotamia and have continued it with few interruptions from that time to this. Numerous cities have been excavated and careful study

has been made of their remains. Each city excavated has increased our skill in the technique of excavation and in our ability to interpret finds correctly. Much has been learned about ancient fortifications, temples, palaces, and so forth. Comparative study of the materials has added much to our knowledge, but to the Bible student even greater interest attaches to the many thousands of clay tablets that have been dug up and placed in museums in many parts of the world. Mesopotamia is remote from the scene of most of the actual events of the Scripture, and consequently the material remains from Mesopotamia, important as they are for the study of ancient history and culture, and interesting as they are intrinsically, are not nearly as important to the Bible student as the literary remains. In this article we will therefore not take the time to look at the excavations in detail, but will spend most of our time on the written material.

C. History of Decipherment And Study of the Languages

1. Decipherment

The key to the reading of cuneiform came, not from Mesopotamia, but from Persia. In 1765 Carsten Niebuhr, a Danish traveler, visited Persepolis, the ancient capital of Persia, and copied a number of inscriptions that were chiseled on the stone walls of the great palaces of the ancient Persian kings. His copies were studied by various European scholars. A young German named G. F. Grotefend was able to put them together and make a substantial start on the decipherment of cuneiform writing. Afterwards, a similar start was made independently by an Englishman, Henry C. Rawlinson, who, as a young army officer, was sent to Persia in 1833 to assist in the reorganization of the Persian army. There he saw the great

Persian inscriptions high up on the mountains near Hamadan and began to study them. Most important was the Behistun inscription of Darius I. About five hundred feet above the plain many lines of large cuneiform signs had been chiseled on the face of the rock, next to a picture of the victorious Darius with many conquered rebels tied together at his feet. The inscription contained three sets of lines, and Rawlinson assumed that these must represent three languages. One set had about 30 different signs which occurred and recurred. The second set of lines, which was somewhat shorter, had about a hundred different characters, while the third, which was still shorter, had far more. It was a good guess that the simpler writing was an alphabetic system and that it represented the ancient Persian language. Since a later form of Persian, in a different kind of writing, was already known, it was possible to make a start at interpreting the first set of lines. In 1846 Rawlinson published a full interpretation of the Persian column of the great Behistun inscription. On the assumption that the second column (Elamite), and the third column (Babylonian) had the same meaning as the first, the three columns were compared, and by 1851 a good start had been made in the interpretation of the Babylonian part of the Behistun inscription.

It was found that often a number of characters in the Persian inscription would be parallel to only one character in the Babylonian, and the conclusion was reached that often one Babylonian sign would represent an entire word. It was determined on further study that there were also signs that represented vowels but none that represented a consonant alone. However, there were many signs that represented a consonant followed or preceded by a vowel, and others that would represent a combina-

tion of consonant-vowel-consonant. Often the same sign would be required by the context to be read in different ways in different combinations. As the Behistun inscription and other inscriptions were studied, scholars came to the decision that one particular sign could represent the syllables *kal, rib, lab,* or *dan,* depending on the context. Another sign could represent the word *limu,* "thousand," the syllable *shi* or the syllable *lim.* If this particular sign should occur twice in succession, it might stand for *shi-shi,* for *lim-lim,* for *shi-lim,* or for *lim-shi,* or the combination might indicate the word *abiktu,* "overthrow." The appalling complexity of the system led many to doubt that the key to its interpretation had actually been found. In 1856 four outstanding students of cuneiform happened to be in London at the same time. The trustees of the British Museum gave each of them a copy of a new inscription of the Assyrian conqueror, Tiglath-Pileser (II Kings 16:7-10), which had not yet been published. Each of the four men worked on it individually, and then presented his conclusions, indicating what parts seemed to him to be certain, and what parts seemed to be obscure. When the interpretations were opened, it was found that the four scholars had agreed in marking essentially the same things as quite clear, and on these their interpretations were just about identical. They also agreed as to the sections marked obscure, and on these their interpretations varied. This agreement was accepted as proof that the decipherment had been successful, and that the key to reading ancient Babylonian was at hand. Soon, bas-reliefs were found in the palaces of Assyrian kings, picturing events in the lives of these monarchs, with an inscription underneath. Reading the inscription without ever seeing the picture, and then comparing the writing with the picture, it was quite apparent that the method of interpretation was indeed correct, and that the complex cuneiform system had really been deciphered. Still later additional bilingual texts were found.

2. The Cuneiform Writing

As mentioned above, cuneiform writing is writing in wedge-shaped characters. This came about because a stylus, which somewhat resembles a small screwdriver, was pressed into a clay tablet, with one end pressed slightly deeper than the other, so as to make a wedge-shaped mark. By combinations of these marks, many different types of signs could be made. Cuneiform writing, like the hieroglyphics, originally began with pictures; however, in most cases the resemblance to the original picture soon disappeared because of the unsuitability of this type of marking for making recognizable likenesses, and in time it was no longer remembered that the sign had ever stood for a particular picture. Originally, cuneiform was written from top to bottom; soon, however, for greater convenience in writing, the tablet was turned sideways to the left, so that the signs went horizontally from left to right, instead of vertically from top to bottom. This made them look still less like the original pictures.

The cuneiform writing was invented by a people called Sumerians, who spoke a language quite unrelated to Babylonian. The Babylonians, or rather, Akkadians, took over the signs from the Sumerians and adapted them to their own language. Hence a sign may sometimes be read either as a Sumerian word (e.g., *dingir*, "god") or as the corresponding Akkadian word (e.g., *ilu*, "god"). There are about one hundred signs that indicate either a vowel alone, a consonant plus a vowel, or a vowel plus a consonant. Quite a number can

represent a combination of consonant plus vowel plus consonant. Most of the signs also have a logographic meaning, that is to say, they can stand for a full word. Sometimes a sign stands for two or three different words that have similar meanings, and one must tell from the context or from the other signs placed next to it, which word it represents. Thus at first sight the cuneiform writing seems to be an extremely complicated system of writing. As over against this, however, it should be noted that it indicates vowels as well as consonants—a real advantage over the Egyptian writing. Indication of vowels is a great help in the understanding of the writing and of the language it represents. Cuneiform was used for thousands of years, and the signs underwent many changes, so that in different periods there is considerable difference, though relationships can generally be observed. The earliest cuneiform inscriptions that were worked out came from Assyrian kings; consequently the Assyrian forms came to be accepted by modern scholars as normative, and the signs are usually arranged in lists according to this order, even though it is quite different from that of the forms used in earlier and later periods.

Unlike the hieroglyphics, which were normally used only to represent one language, the cuneiform came to be employed for quite a variety of languages, over a wide area, wherever it was convenient to use clay tablets.

3. Akkadian

The language that is most commonly written in cuneiform, and from which we have the greatest number of tablets—hundreds of thousands in fact—was at first called Assyrian. Later it was realized that Assyrian is a dialect of Babylonian with certain special peculiarities; therefore the name Assyrian has been given up as a designation for the language and is retained only for one of its dialects. Many of the tablets written in this language come from Babylon and the cities associated with it, but others are from a period before the founding of Babylon, and come from people who had as their leading center the city of Akkad, or Agade. From this name modern scholars have formed the term Akkadian (or Accadian), which is today used to designate the language as a whole. Akkadian was used for over 2500 years in writings by people spread over quite a wide area. The language is a Semitic language, that is to say, it is related to Hebrew, Aramaic, Arabic, and Ethiopic, and shares many of the peculiarities of these languages. Anyone having a good start in one of these languages will easily recognize many Akkadian words. As a language it is probably easier than the Egyptian, particularly with the advantage that is secured through having the vowels represented as well as the consonants, and this to some extent makes up for the greater complexity of the signs and the greater difficulty of memorizing them. Many scholars in various countries have busied themselves with studying the Akkadian language. Its extensive literature is extremely varied, including detailed historical texts, lengthy law codes, magical texts and incantations, legal texts, contracts, lists of all sorts of property, and a tremendous variety of personal letters.

There are a number of periods in which the Akkadian language varies considerably. The earliest, which preceded the rise of Babylon, is designated as the Old Akkadian. The next is the Old Babylonian period, when scholars, especially at the city of Nippur, studied the writing and the language in order to make it more systematic, and prepared dictionaries, grammars, and lists

of forms, which have been extremely helpful to modern scholars. The language is more regular and systematic at this period than at any time before or since. During the latter part of the second millennium B.C., two varying dialects, called Middle Babylonian and Middle Assyrian, occur in quite a variety of tablets, especially legal documents. Then comes the later Assyrian period, the time of the supremacy of the great kings of Assyria. From this period many historical and administrative documents have been preserved. It is followed by the Neo-Babylonian period, the time of the renewed greatness of Babylon, in which a type of writing rather different from Assyrian is used, and again there is a great variety of materials. Modern scholars have extensively studied various periods of Akkadian, writing grammars and dictionaries of them. There is still much work to be done in this field, but tremendous progress has been made. A good survey of the various types of Akkadian literature in translation can be found in *Ancient Near Eastern Texts Related to the Old Testament*, edited by James B. Pritchard, which contains translations of various types of documents by a number of well-known scholars.

4. Sumerian

Before scholars had gone far in the study of Akkadian, they began to find signs used to represent something quite different from their usual meaning. It was at first thought that these signs represented a sort of code-language in which ideas were presented in an abbreviated form. However, the suggestion was soon made that instead it represented an earlier language, parts of which were still used in writing the later language, much as Latin phrases and particularly abbreviations (e.g., i.e., etc.), occur in English. This was proven to be the case when whole documents in the Sumerian language were discovered, when texts were found giving lists of Sumerian words with translations into Akkadian, and when, eventually, it became possible to draw up a whole history of many parts of the Sumerian culture. It was evident that the Sumerian was a distinct language, antedating the writing of the Akkadian, a language which in its grammatical features is entirely distinct from Akkadian, having perhaps less similarity to it than Chinese has to English. The writing was taken over from the Sumerians by the Akkadians, and continued to be used for certain official purposes right up to the end of the pre-Christian era, long after Sumerian itself was a completely dead language.

5. Akkadian as a *lingua franca*

In 1887 a peasant woman in S Egypt happened upon a large group of clay tablets with cuneiform marks on them. They were unlike anything she had ever seen before. Her friends took them to Cairo and tried to sell them, but they were unfamiliar to scholars of Egyptology, and it was some time before a student from Mesopotamia happened to see them and recognized immediately that these tablets, though found far S in Egypt, were written in the Akkadian language and the cuneiform writing. This set of tablets, most of which are either in the British Museum or in the Berlin Museum, are known as the El Amarna documents because they were found at the capital of Akhenaton in Egypt. Reference has already been made to them (II.D.5). They show that Akkadian had come to be used for correspondence between people who spoke entirely different languages just as French has become a primary language for diplomacy in modern times.

There was also the advantage that clay tablets were very convenient for carrying about on diplomatic missions.

In N Mesopotamia a group of people speaking an entirely different language, known as Hurrian, found it convenient to use the Akkadian language for all their legal documents and court cases. The town where more of these tablets have been found than anywhere else was a place called Nuzi near the modern Kerkuk. The Nuzi documents have a grammar that is quite often confused since their writers were actually thinking in the Hurrian language. They provide many interesting insights into the lives and activities of a group very distinct from the Akkadian-speaking peoples. For their relation to the Bible, see below (III.D.5).

6. Other Uses of Cuneiform

Many languages other than Akkadian have also been written in cuneiform writing. Thus the Hittite language from Asia Minor, written in the cuneiform writing, throws light on an entirely different area of history, though having some contacts with the Assyrians and Babylonians and also with the Egyptians. A number of cuneiform texts have also been found that are written in the Hurrian language.

D. Survey of the History of Mesopotamia

1. Prehistoric

Many cities that have been excavated go back to a time long before the invention of writing. We cannot hope to know as much about these times as about those from which writing has been found, but yet a good deal can be told about their life. There seems to have been a rather leisurely period when most of the implements were made out of stone and people had time to make them very carefully and to show considerable artistic sense in their workmanship. In some ways there was a rather high civilization. From the study of the pottery (or dishes), various races have been differentiated as having been prominent in Mesopotamia at different periods. The study of prehistoric Mesopotamia is a fascinating one, but has comparatively little contact with the Bible and hence is only to a slight extent properly included under Biblical Archaeology.

The prehistoric period ends with two events which seem to have occurred about the same time. One of these was the discovery of how to smelt copper, thus making it possible to make a great number of weapons much more quickly than could be done before. This gave a tremendous advantage to every city that acquired this skill and resulted in a series of wars that left desolation throughout most of Mesopotamia. The other event that occurred at about the same time was the invention of writing.

2. The Sumerian Period

The Sumerians, who called themselves the Blackheaded People, spoke a language unrelated to any other known language. There have been many guesses as to where they came from. Most likely they entered Mesopotamia by boat. They were a very practical people. The writing which they invented fits their language quite well, and is about as ill-adapted to Akkadian as the Latin system of writing is to our English language. The Sumerians were probably always a minority in a land in which the Akkadian people were more numerous, but with their practical skill they controlled the region for quite a time. Their writings include myths and epics, some of which have been thought to have a relation to stories in the Bible.

3. The Old Akkadian Period

After a time, the Akkadian-speaking people gained their freedom from the Sumerians and established themselves in control. Some of their leaders were quite powerful, and conquering expeditions went as far W as the Mediterranean Sea. The Old Akkadian Period lasted a few centuries, and we have a considerable number of pictures, monuments, and writings from this period, but far less is known of it than of most of the later periods.

4. The Early Babylonian Period

By a series of wars and by clever diplomatic dealings, the city of Babylon, peopled by W Semites, got control over all of Mesopotamia and also over quite a number of the neighboring regions. The sixth king of the first dynasty of Babylon, who succeeded in making most of these conquests, was named Hammurabi. Hammurabi put up a great law code in the central square of Babylon so that anyone who thought himself wronged could come to the central square and read the law and know what his rights were. The law is a very extensive one, primarily a code of civil and criminal law, rather than of religious law. It has many points of contact with the laws of the Pentateuch. The time of Hammurabi was a time of great literary activity. Priests in the temple of Nippur worked on the organization of the language and of the writing to make it more suitable. The language is much purer at this time than ever before or after. The grammar is followed more consistently and the case endings are used more correctly than at any other period.

The city of Mari, on the upper Euphrates, was in league with Babylon for many years, but was conquered and destroyed near the end of Hammurabi's long reign. Excavations at Mari have uncovered the remains of great capital buildings, throwing much light on the life of the period. Thousands of clay tablets were found, largely consisting of administrative letters giving us a vivid picture of the culture and of the political vicissitudes of the times.

5. The Remainder of The Second Millennium B.C.

The second millennium B.C. was a time of great upheavals and movements of nations. A mountain people, the Cassites, swept into Mesopotamia, overcame Babylon, and set up a Cassite regime which imitated the forms of the Babylonian rulers for over a century. Great numbers of Hurrians settled in N. Mesopotamia and in Syria, and took over the Akkadian language for their official documents. It is a difficult period to understand fully, because of the great variety of people, languages, and customs. We have already mentioned the tablets from Nuzi, a place that was conquered by Assyria about 1400 B.C. and remained buried and forgotten until its discovery in 1926. These Hurrian peoples in N. Mesopotamia seem to have been closely related to the peoples among whom Jacob visited when he was with his uncle Laban. Consequently, there are interesting contacts between these tablets and the customs and culture reflected in the story of the patriarchs in Genesis (see article on TERAPHIM).

6. The Assyrian Period

We now come to a period that has many specific contacts with Biblical history. The Assyrian kings carried on a constant policy of aggression that made them a menace to Israel for a long time. In 721 B.C. they conquered the N kingdom, and they remained a constant danger to Judah until 604 B.C., when the Assyrian empire itself was con-quered by the Babylonians under Nebuchadnezzar. For details of the history of the Assyrian kings, see the article on ASSYRIA. The book of Nahum vividly portrays the downfall of the Assyrian empire.

7. The Neo-Babylonian Period

Although Babylon had been politically of secondary importance for many centuries, it had continued to have great importance as a cultural, religious, and commercial center. After the downfall of the Assyrian Empire, Babylon experienced a brilliant period of glory, that lasted for about 70 years. Its great king, Nebuchadnezzar, extended his conquests as far as Egypt. He changed the face of his capital city of Babylon, erecting many great buildings there and in other parts of Mesopotamia. The extensiveness of his building operations, and his pride in them, is illustrated by the fact that over a million bricks have been excavated, each of them stamped with the name and titles of Nebuchadnezzar the great king. It is therefore easy to picture him as described in Daniel 4:30, where he says, "Is not this great Babylon that I have built?"

The empire established by Nebuchadnezzar continued through a number of reigns (for list of the kings and their dates, see article BABYLON). Its last king was named Nabonidus. Nabonidus associated his son Belshazzar with him as king, as inferred in Daniel 5. Belshazzar was killed at the time of the Persian conquest of Babylon.

8. The Persian Period

With the conquest of Babylon by the Persians, Mesopotamian independence ended. Cyrus the great, at first a subject king under the Medes, had established his supremacy over them and then had led the Medes and Persians on to conquer all of Asia Minor and the regions around Babylon, then to conquer Babylon and put an end to the Babylonian empire. The speed of his conquest is vividly illustrated in the predictions in Daniel 8:3,4 (cf. v. 20), and in Isaiah 41:2, 3, 25; and 45:1, 2. Cyrus was succeeded by his son, Cambyses, who conquered Egypt. He was followed by another very great ruler, Darius I. The Persian control lasted over 200 years. It was a time of comparative peace and prosperity. Although the Persian kings ruled with an absolute despotism, they gave their people a large measure of individual freedom. It was, on the whole, an enlightened monarchy.

9. The Hellenistic Period

As predicted in Daniel 8:5-8 (cf. v. 21-22), Alexander the Great moved against the Persian Empire. In 331 B.C. he conquered Darius III and established his own domain over the whole region formerly held by the Persians. His early death resulted in struggles among his followers which ended in the division of his empire into several sections, Ptolemy seizing Egypt, and Seleucus seizing Babylon and the surrounding areas. From each of these proceeded a dynasty that ruled a large territory, the borders of which shifted from time to time in the succeeding period of more than two centuries. During this time the Greek language came to be widely used, and Greek customs and culture assumed a dominant position in many parts of the Near East, though the cuneiform writing, like the Egyptian hieroglyphics, continued to be used to some extent.

E. Relations of Mesopotamian Archaelogy to the OT

The relations of Mesopotamian archaeology to the OT are very extensive and extremely varied. They relate to many different periods of time. There are many obvious relationships and many that are not so obvious. It is likely that there is more material at present available from Mesopotamia that directly bears on the OT, than from all other archaeological sources put together. We shall look first at a few of the high points of relationship.

1. Genesis 1-11

There is nothing in Mesopotamian archaeology throwing light upon the historical events described in Genesis 1-11. The historical connections begin with the time of Abraham. However, certain scholars have held that practically everything in these chapters was taken over from or based upon a Babylonian prototype. In most cases examination of this alleged derivation proves it to be highly questionable. The form of writing, or even the mode of expression, may sometimes have been influenced by Mesopotamian culture. But the particular stories that are alleged to have similarities to the accounts of creation, of the Fall, etc., are in most cases very different from the Biblical material. However, there is one striking exception: the story of the Flood.

The Biblical account of the creation was revealed by God to the writer, and has little similarity to any creation story in Babylon, despite assertions to the contrary. (For further discussion see article, CREATION.) Such similarities as exist are of general nature and would be almost certain to be found in any story of creation. No man saw the creation, and so many centuries elapsed between creation and the time of the writing of the Babylonian literature that one would hardly expect that any details that the first men might have known would be remembered. The situation is quite different as regards the Babylonian story of the Flood, which has many remarkable similarities to the Biblical story, not only in general features, as might easily be true in any story of a great flood even if it arose entirely independently, but also in quite a number of details. There are striking differences of detail, but there are enough obvious similarities in details of an incidental nature to make it difficult to think that the two stories are not in some way related. This is, however, just what one might expect. The story of the Flood would have been well known to Noah's descendants. Even after they turned away from God, such a striking event, comparatively recent in their history, would not be easily forgotten. In the course of time it became confused and corrupted so that much that was erroneous crept into the Babylonian story, and yet enough was retained that was identical with the true facts to leave a number of remarkable similarities to the account that has been correctly preserved for us in Genesis 6-9. (For further details, see article FLOOD.)

2. The Period of the Patriarchs

The Biblical story of the patriarchs begins with Abram's coming from Mesopotamia, and many details can be compared with Mesopotamian sources. Ur was a great city long before the time of Abraham, as was also Haran in N Mesopotamia. Many of the customs that find expression in the life of Abraham have a close similarity to those prescribed in the laws of Hammurabi. The customs of Jacob have marked similarity to items found in the Nuzi tablets, reflecting the life of N Mesopotamia at this period.

**3. The Period of the Kings—
The Assyrian Period**

During the latter part of the history of the Israelite kingdom, the Assyrian empire was coming more and more to the front, until it became the decisive factor in the history of Israel and of Judah. Here the contacts are numerous. Assyrian kings are mentioned in the Bible and Israelite kings are mentioned in Assyrian records.

4. The Neo-Babylonian Period

The Kingdom of Judah was taken captive not by Assyria but by its successor, the Neo-Babylonian Empire. The book of Daniel reflects the background of the reign of Nebuchadnezzar, and there are many points at which Mesopotamian archaeology throws light on the Biblical narrative, offering help in its interpretation and giving much valuable corroborative material.

**5. Relation to
General Corroboration**

The Biblical account shows Abram, because of his trust in God, leaving a land of high civilization for one that he did not know. This is generally corroborated by the picture that archaeology gives of the great ancient culture land of Mesopotamia from which he came, a land whose traditions exerted much influence over the customs of the patriarchs, even in distant Palestine. Mesopotamia was a factor, though not a dominant one, in Palestine in the years between the time of the patriarchs and of the later Israelite kingdom. Thus we find Achan in Joshua 7:21 stealing "a goodly Babylonish garment." A century after the division of the kingdom, Mesopotamia begins to loom as a vital force, and Mesopotamian archaeology shows the rise of Assyria as a powerful aggressor at this time. The picture contained in the book of Nahum and elsewhere of the terror that the Assyrians inspired is well illustrated by the accounts given out by Assyrian kings, in which they gloat over the policy of "calculated frightfulness" that they adopted in order to scare those whom they had conquered into remaining loyal to them. The Biblical description of the carrying off of multitudes of people into captivity in distant lands fits with the Mesopotamian evidence which shows that the Assyrian kings invented a policy of attempting to strengthen their control over their empires by moving whole populations from one section to another. The Bible says that Cyrus reversed this policy, allowing the Jews to return to their homeland, and this change of policy is also corroborated by cuneiform records.

6. Relation to Special Corroboration

It would require a volume to consider all the specific points that should be considered under this head. Most of them will be treated under the names of the persons concerned. One special matter should be indicated here. There are many individuals mentioned in the Bible whose names are also found in cuneiform records. Proper names are among the most difficult matters to pass on accurately, as it is very easy to make errors in copying them, particularly when they are foreign names. The LXX was translated from the OT about 200 B.C. and has been copied and re-copied, as the Hebrew manuscripts have been. When we look at the proper names in the LXX, we find that at many points they are greatly changed, while the Hebrew Bible, which was considered by its copyists as a sacred book, has preserved them far more accurately. The Assyrian and Babylonian records give some of these names as they were written down at the time, and thus enable us to note the amazing degree of accuracy in the preservation of names that was attained by the Hebrew text. Even more striking is the way in which

the names of the rulers of Mesopotamia and Israel are arranged. They occur in the Bible in the same combinations and in the same chronological arrangement as in the Mesopotamian records, something that could never have happened by chance.

7. Relation to Interpretation

Babylonian material is of help in the interpretation of the Bible at a great number of points. There are many references to Babylonian and Assyrian kings, and to Mesopotamian matters and customs. Archaeological material makes these far easier to understand. An interesting illustration occurs in Nahum 1:12, where the AV reads: "though they be quiet, and likewise many, yet thus shall they be cut down." The ARV says, "though they be in full strength, and likewise many, even so shall they be cut down." The RSV reads, "though they be strong and many, they shall be cut off." It is hard to get much sense out of the reading of the AV. Why should the fact that they are quiet constitute a reason for difficulty in conquering them? The other two make good sense but are a guess rather than a translation of Hebrew. The word translated "quiet," "in full strength," or, in the RSV, simply "strong," is defined in our leading Hebrew dictionary as meaning "complete," "safe," "at peace." The word which two versions render "likewise" (and the RSV omits altogether) really means "so," or "therefore." No one of the versions renders it this way, because it would not seem to make sense in the context. RSV inserts a footnote, "Heb. uncertain." It is plain that no one of the versions has the real thought of the verse. Commentaries have made guesses differing widely from one another. Mesopotamian studies now enable us to know the true meaning. God is here predicting the destruction of the great Assyrian power, the theme to which the entire book of Nahum is devoted. At this point he simply quotes an Assyrian legal phrase, *shalmu kenu,* which occurs in hundreds of Assyrian contracts and legal documents to indicate several and joint responsibility for the carrying out of an obligation. To anyone living at the time and familiar with Assyrian customs, the phrase conveyed as much meaning as a page of discussion. It declares that even though the Assyrians should stand together, every one with his shoulder to the task, carrying out to the full his national obligations, nevertheless God will break through their ranks and destroy their power. The phrase is quite incomprehensible apart from the Assyrian background which archaeology has revealed to us. In turn, it becomes an interesting and remarkable corroboration of the accuracy of the Biblical narrative.

8. Relation to Derivation

We have already mentioned the relation of the stories in Genesis 1-11 to the idea of derivation of Biblical ideas from Mesopotamian sources (III.E.1). This idea was brought to the fore by Prof. Friedrich Delitzsch in his "Babel and the Bible" lectures, given in 1902 and 1903 in Berlin. In these lectures he recognized that Mesopotamian discoveries had shown many historical and cultural features of the Biblical account to be remarkably accurate, but went on to assert that these discoveries also prove that the religious and cultural ideas of the Bible are simply an inferior borrowing from a superior cultural and religious environment found in Mesopotamia. Great excitement was aroused by Delitzsch's lectures, but most of the theories he advanced have not stood the test of time. Scholars immediately pointed out many flaws, and

others have subsequently come to light. Yet many of his ideas are uncritically accepted in liberal circles today, and unfounded theories of derivation are sometimes widely used for discrediting the dependability of the Biblical accounts.

Another area of alleged derivation is the field of law. At one time it was held that the Pentateuchal laws were far too advanced to have been written at the time of Moses. Discovery of the Code of Hammurabi proved that a much more complex code than that in the Pentateuch had been promulgated centuries before the time of Moses. The next step was to allege that the Pentateuchal laws were borrowed from the Code of Hammurabi (cf. III.D.4). Such dependence of one upon the other, however, can easily be shown not to be the case. There may be places where the civil laws of the Pentateuch reflect civil laws that were known in Mesopotamia, but the basic emphasis of the Pentateuchal law is primarily religious and very different from the basically secular emphasis of the Code of Hammurabi.

Mesopotamian study constitutes a fruitful field for the Bible student. Many ill-founded theories and superficial interpretations have been disseminated in relation to this material. After they have been carefully sifted and the superficial and the unwarranted have been eliminated, there still remains a tremendous amount of material throwing light upon the Bible, showing it to be remarkably accurate in general, and specifically corroborating it at many points.

A. Syria

The region immediately N and NE of Palestine looms large in the history of the Divided Kingdom. Properly, this region should be

IV. Other Areas Outside Palestine thought of in two sections, separated from one another by the Lebanon Mountains. The region along the Mediterranean Sea directly N of Palestine is now an independent country called Lebanon, while that further inland, centering around Damascus, is today called Syria. These two sections have developed rather differently, though there have been many interrelations between them. Three great cities of the Lebanon region, Tyre, Sidon, and Byblos, have been important in various ways in Biblical history. Tyre and Sidon have often been united, with one or the other of them assuming the leadership.

Lebanon and, to some extent, Syria, had the advantage of receiving papyrus from Egypt in trade, which made it much easier for them to make records than for the people of Mesopotamia, but at the same time caused these records to disintegrate within a few decades. Very little cuneiform has been found in this region from the time of the Divided Kingdom, though many cuneiform tablets have been found from an earlier period. The annals of the Assyrian kings contain many references to events and personages in Syria, particularly in the Damascus area, and these are important for the study of special corroboration. A few Aramaic inscriptions have been found on monuments in the region of Syria. One of these corroborates the name of the king of Damascus mentioned in I Kings 15:18, and in addition gives evidence of the proselyting activities of the Sidonians for their god Melkart, who was called Baal (or Master) in I Kings 16:31 and the following chapters. The proselyting done by the priests of Baal in Israel at about this time made necessary the work of Elijah and Elisha. So this is a most interesting general corroboraton of these activities.

Perhaps the most interesting discovery from this region was the finding of the Ras Shamra inscriptions. In 1929 French excavators began to excavate the promontory of Ras Shamra on the N portion of the Lebanon coast. Impressive buildings came to light with some very interesting paintings, a certain number of tablets written in Akkadian cuneiform, and a large group of tablets in an entirely new type of writing, with signs that looked like cuneiform but that could not be read by ordinary methods. Since there were not more than 30 different signs, it was a good guess that it was some sort of alphabetic system. Professor H. Bauer, a German scholar who had worked on decipherment of enemy codes in World War I, was able to interpret a number of the signs. The paper in which he gave his attempted decipherment reached the American School of Oriental Research in Jerusalem, and Dr. W. F. Albright, the then Director of the School, took it over to the French Ecole Biblique and showed it to Professor E. Dhorme, who had worked with the French army deciphering enemy codes. Dhorme had already been studying these tablets and had worked out quite a number of the letters. Putting together those he had worked out and the ones that Bauer had worked out, the foundation was laid for reading this new kind of writing. It was based on the cuneiform type of writing, but written by people familiar with the Canaanite alphabet, who had made an artificial alphabet of their own. The tablets were in a language closely related to Hebrew, and many of them contained epics and other religious literature of the ancient Canaanites.

The name of the city at that time was shown to have been Ugarit; so the language is now called Ugaritic. The study of the Ugaritic tablets throws much light on Canaanite religion prior to the coming of the Israelites. The material has been avidly studied by those who wish to show that Israelite religion is taken over from the Canaanites. However, most of the alleged relationships of this type disappear on close examination. It is true that there is considerable cultural relationship and occasionally forms of expression are common to both, but the religious ideas are actually very different. The study of Ugaritic is a very extensive study. Possession of this large body of religious material, in a language so close to Biblical Hebrew, is sure to give valuable help in the understanding of Hebrew words and expressions. Much remains to be done, not only in examining the Ugaritic evidence to determine the true situation in regard to the many statements that have been made about derivation of Biblical material from Canaanite sources, but also in gleaning its valuable help for Biblical interpretation.

B. The Hittites

There was a time when the very existence of the Hittites was doubted. However, it has now been proven that they were a very great people, able to fight with the Egyptians on even terms over a period of a century and eventually to make a treaty of alliance with them. In 1906 Boghaz-keuoi in Asia Minor, the Hittite capital, was excavated, and many tablets were unearthed, written in cuneiform script but in the Hittite language, which proved to be related to the Indo-European group of languages. The relation of the Hittites to Biblical history is not great. Some of the OT references to the Hittites probably refer to Hurrians, rather than Hittites (see article on HURRIANS).

C. Persia

We have noticed that the first clues to the interpretation of cuneiform came from Persia. Here Darius had his great palace at Persepolis. The Persian kings had another great palace at Susa, which was excavated by the French in 1884-6. The antiquities brought from Susa to Paris have been deposited in two large rooms in the Louvre and a model of the palace has been constructed. Many of the events in the book of Esther took place in "Shushan the palace." With the model before us it is easy to see where each of these events occurred. In fact, there is hardly an event described in the OT whose material surroundings can be so vividly and accurately restored from actual excavations as these details in the book of Esther.

Objection has been made to the actuality of the story of Haman's decree in Esther 3:5-15, because of the long interval that was allowed the Jews before the arrival of their day of destruction. Esther 3:7 (cf. v. 13) says that "they cast Pur, that is, the lot," in order to determine the time. A most interesting instance of general corroboration is provided by the fact that the French excavators found in the mound at Susa one of the dice that were thus used to determine events. Careful tests showed that this die might be thrown even scores of times before it would stop on the desired number.

While there is not a great deal of actual material from Persia that has definite relation to Biblical statements, the little that we have is very interesting.

Mention should be made of the claim that important features of Biblical teaching have been derived from Persian religion. The sources for knowledge of the history of ancient Zoroastrianism are rather obscure and theories differ widely. Here is an area where study of Persian antiquity should yield fruitful results as regards a vital question of derivation, particularly since some of the religious aspects that are said to have entered Judaism from Persia occupy an important position in the NT as well.

D. South Arabia

A great number of short inscriptions have been found in S Arabia, showing the early existence of a high civilization. Great irrigation works were built at an early period. This was probably the home of the Queen of Sheba, who came to see the wisdom of Solomon (I Kings 10:1-13).

A. Difference from Egypt and Mesopotamia

Although far more events in OT history took place in Palestine than anywhere else, we are treating Palestine last because archaeolo-
V. Archaeology of Palestine gy there secured a firm foundation considerably later than in either Egypt or Mesopotamia. It is easy to see why it would be harder to get a solid footing in Palestinian archaeology than in these other two regions. They were lands of tremendous fertility, with great rivers bringing to them the means of almost constant prosperity. Palestine had no such advantage. The River Jordan is in a deep valley far removed from most of the historic areas of Palestine. It is an obstacle to be crossed, and not to any great extent a source of water or fertility. Comparatively few of the important events of Biblical history took place in the Jordan Valley, and this area was a prosperous region only during the very earliest period and never again in Biblical times. In most of Palestine prosperity was dependent on rainfall. This prosperity never reached the heights attained in Egypt and in Mesopotamia, where the monarchs were able to erect colossal temples and palaces, and to force thousands of people to build them great memorials, with inscriptions carved in the solid rock. From a political viewpoint Palestine was never in a class with the other regions.

There is an even more important reason why we have less material from Palestine that is vital for archaeology than from Egypt or Mesopotamia. This reason lies partly in the nature of the climate and partly in the location. The climate is not nearly as dry as in Egypt, and materials crumble much faster. Even when buried, papyrus is not apt to last many centuries, except in the very dry sections of the wilderness beside the Dead Sea. A few clay tablets have been found in Palestine, but their number is not great. It was far simpler to write on papyrus, which was available because of the nearness of Egypt.

Probably there was a great amount of writing done in Palestine at all periods, but being on papyrus most of it disintegrated very rapidly. Occasionally, lack of papyrus made it necessary to write on clay tablets or to scratch records on pieces of broken pottery, and this accounts for most of the little writing from OT times that has been found in Palestine. This scarcity of written materials is a great hindrance. Other methods than study of written material have had to be utilized to get the very important help for Biblical archaeology that has come from Palestine.

B. Exploration to 1914— The Vital Principles Discovered

In Palestine the period before 1914 was not extremely productive of valuable results in Biblical archaeology. Many times as much has been learned since the First World War as before. Yet the foundations of all subsequent progress in Palestinian archaeology were laid before 1914, and credit for them belongs particularly to two men: Prof. Edward Robinson and Sir William Flinders Petrie.

Among the Christians of the first three centuries after Christ, there seems to have been little interest in the details of Palestinian geography. Christians were oriented toward the return of Christ to set up His glorious kingdom of peace and happiness. They spread over the earth witnessing to their Master and pointing people toward the coming age rather than toward the events of the past (I Thess. 1:9-10). Little effort was made by Christians during those years to preserve the memory of the places where Biblical events had occurred. This was especially unfortunate for our knowledge of Palestine since the Jews were not in a position to make up the lack. Multitudes of Jews perished in A.D. 70, when Jerusalem was destroyed by the Romans. In A.D. 132-5 the rebellion of Bar Cochba was savagely put down, and Hadrian established a pagan city on the ruins of Jerusalem with orders that no Jew could come within ten miles of the city. Thus these three centuries were a time when it was easy to lose all knowledge of the locations where Biblical events had occurred.

A change came with the reign of Constantine, the first Christian emperor. Interest in learning about the region where the Savior had lived was stimulated when Constantine's pious mother, Helena, visited Palestine and tried to find the places where events in the life of Christ had occurred. Helena was no trained geographer and many of her results are highly questionable. Yet traditions were established by her that continued for centuries, many of them right up to the present time. More productive for our knowledge of Palestine was the work of the church historian Eusebius, who wrote his *Onomasticon*, a list of Palestinian proper names with an attempt to identify their sites. Eusebius sought out traditions regarding Biblical places, preserved such names as had lasted up to his day, and included information about Roman roads and other important data that would otherwise be completely lost to us. A century later Jerome, the learned translator of the Vulgate, translated Eusebius' book into Latin with comments of his own.

During the greater part of the Middle Ages the Holy Land was held by hostile Moslems, but many pilgrims made brief visits to that region, and some of them wrote descriptions of their experiences. Some of the pilgrim accounts that have been preserved are of value, but in most cases their importance for the understanding of Palestine is slight.

The new day dawned with Edward Robinson, an American theological professor. After graduate study in Germany under the best geographical and linguistic scholarship of the time, Robinson taught Biblical subjects for many years and took a great interest in locating Palestinian places. Fnding the material on the subject very scanty and often not at all dependable, he determined to make a trip to Palestine to investigate for himself. In 1838 he went to Egypt and there was joined by Eli Smith, a missionary who had spent years in becoming familiar with Arabic language and customs. The two of them travelled for six weeks in Palestine, and Robinson added hundreds of names to the map. He applied excellent scientific methodology to checking the location of Biblical places and criticizing arguments that might not be valid. The result is that far more of his determinations have lasted than of any of the explorers who succeeded him in following years. In 1851 Robinson made another brief trip through Palestine continuing the excellent work that he had done before.

The publication of Robinson's efforts gave a spur to Palestinian study, and soon actual excavation began, but the point had not yet been reached where such excavation could be entirely profitable. The Palestinian Exploration Fund, founded in England in 1865, laid out an ambitious but premature program of excavation to determine vital problems in Palestinian history. More fruitful was its work in sending trained engineers to make a survey of W Palestine (1871-8). This map formed a basis for decades of subsequent study. Unfortunately, the map was made before the work of Flinders Petrie, which, if known, would have resulted in adding certain very important data which were not generally included in the otherwise very excellent map that was prepared.

In 1890 the Palestine Exploration Fund asked Flinders Petrie, already a veteran in Egyptian exploration and excavation, to excavate for it at a place in SW Palestine which was thought to be the site of ancient Lachish. Forty years later the identification was proven to be incorrect, but this in no way detracts from the importance of Petrie's work, for in a few weeks he laid the foundation upon which all subsequent Palestinian study rests to a large extent. This consisted in pointing out the great importance of two factors, the "tell" and the use of pottery for dating.

Petrie observed that in ancient Palestine the number of places suitable for the founding of cities was limited by two necessary factors: (1) a good spring must be available, and (2) the location must be suited for defense against enemy attack. This meant that most towns were built on hills, and that they were usually surrounded by strong walls. Even in peace time the height of a city kept growing, since refuse was simply thrown into the street, and when old houses were destroyed, new ones were built on top of the ruins. Eventually the city would be attacked by an enemy strong enough to destroy it. The conqueror might simply leave the town in a state of ruin, its people having fled or having been killed. Then either the enemy or someone else would desire to build a new town in the area. Looking for a place that could be easily defended and that had a good spring, the selection was quite apt to fall upon the place previously used. So a new city would be built on the ruins, the old walls being to some extent utilized and enlarged, or new walls built above them. Thus cities tended to rise, the city of one period being above the remains of the city of a previous period. Such an artificial hill, covering the remains of ancient cities, is designated as a "tell," using the Arabic word for mound, or hill, and is somewhat like a layer cake, with different layers preserving the remains of occupation at different periods.

Petrie had been asked to excavate Lachish, which was thought to have been at a place called Umm Lakis. He quickly saw that Umm Lakis was merely a late village, not going back into OT times, and transferred his attention to Tell el-Hesy, a conspicuous mound in the neighborhood, thus discovering a matter of prime importance to Palestinian archaeology. Many of the ancient names preserved in Palestine are at villages that do not go back further than the time of Christ. Yet such a town may preserve the name of a place that was important in the time of Abraham. This is because the Romans introduced a measure of safety into Palestine that had usually been unknown before their time. Roman legionaries sought out the bandits and destroyed them, thus establishing such control over the area that people no longer felt the need of strong walls for protection. As each morning they would leave their homes on top of a tell, which might by this time have become quite high, to walk down into the open fields to work during the day, and as they would climb back up the long ascent each evening, they would begin to wonder why this extra effort was necessary. In case after case during the Roman era, people abandoned their old homes and carried the name of their town to a new location down in the plain. The name might continue for centuries in the new location, while somewhere within a few miles a "tell" might stand as a deserted ruin, soon so covered with sand that no one would even remember that a town had ever been there, and bearing a name such as "hill of beans" or "mound of the house of the man who makes the camel run fast." If this discovery had been made 20 years earlier, so that all of these hills with unimportant-sounding names would have been included in the map of Palestine, archaeology would have moved-forward more rapidly than it did.

The second discovery that Petrie made, that of the importance of pottery for dating, was equally vital. It consisted in the application to Palestine of something that he had learned in Egypt while attempting to arrange prehistoric tombs in chronological order. He had observed that pottery (ancient dishes) was used everywhere, ever since it was first invented back in prehistoric times. Pots are easily broken and once broken are extremely difficult to mend. It is usually far simpler to get new ones than to try to mend old ones. No matter how badly pottery is broken up, it is easy to distinguish it from anything else. Wherever people have lived for any length of time, at least a few pieces of broken pottery are sure to be found. Not only does pottery tell whether people have lived at a place or not; it can give an idea of the time when they were there. This is because there are so many ways in which the style of pottery can change from time to time. It can be plain, decorated in one color, or decorated in various colors. It can be decorated with geometrical figures, or with naturalistic pictures. It can have various kinds of bases or of handles. It can be made in many different shapes. The firing can be done in such a way as to produce a very hard, brittle texture, or to produce a softer grade of pottery. There are so many ways in which it can vary from time to time that Petrie had been able to work out a "sequence dating" in Egypt, in which he arranged pottery in the order in which it had been used through a number of prehistoric centuries.

Tel el-Hesy was ideal for the attempt to apply the same principles in Palestine. A little stream had eroded one side of the hill, exposing the edge of successive levels, so that Petrie could move up and down the side of the tell, pulling out pieces of pottery at different points and comparing them. He laid down the principle that pottery could be even more important than writing as a means of dating. It was more than 30 years before the scientific world was altogether ready to accept Petrie's conclusions, but now the importance of pottery is universally recognized. Even before excavating, it is often possible to tell the periods at which a city has been occupied, and this information can be invaluable in determining its identity.

Petrie's work was utilized to a greater or less extent by subsequent explorers and excavators. Some work of fair importance was done before the First World War, but organization of expeditions was not generally as carefully planned as was possible later, and the basis had not yet been laid for most effective excavation. Frequently, excavation was made simply by digging trenches, a method that might promise to yield immediate results but generally failed to provide enough related material for proper understanding. A few men made great efforts to master the science of Palestinian pottery and eventually succeeded in convincing the scholarly world that it is a safe criterion for chronology. When a few clear specimens are available, it is often possible to date something as close as within half a century. For purposes of dating, history has been divided into the various portions of the Stone Age, followed by Early Bronze (about 3000-2000 B.C.), Middle Bronze (about 2000-1500 B.C.), Late Bronze (about 1500-1200 B.C.), Iron I (about 1200-900 B.C.), Iron II (about 900-600 B.C.), and Iron III (about 600-300 B.C.). Later periods are named according to the group that is politically or culturally dominant.

C. Excavation Between the Two World Wars (1919-1939)

1. General Conditions

The period between 1919 and 1939 was a time of great advance in Palestinian archaeology. There are a number of reasons why conditions were far more satisfactory and progress far greater than at any previous period. First of these is the fact that Palestine was now under a British Mandate. When it had been part of the Ottoman Empire, its administration had been largely subject to the whims of local satraps. Now the British Mandate undertook to establish orderly control in every regard, and this made the carrying on of excavation much more satisfactory.

The new government established a Department of Antiquities, headed by a professional archaeologist who had oversight of all archaeological work in the country. Anyone desiring to excavate had to secure permission from the Department, and was required to show that the work would be competently directed. This was important, because once a tell is excavated it can never be done again. As long as it stands untouched, its valuable information about ancient times continues to be preserved. Once it is excavated, whatever has not been learned is gone forever. Each excavation that has been well conducted has given knowledge by means of which the next one can be done still better and can yield still greater results in the increase of our knowledge of ancient times. The Department not only required that an expedition would be directed by properly trained men, it also required evidence that sufficient funds were in hand to carry through to a proper conclusion whatever work was begun. It would require a well-financed organization to excavate a large mound. A small mound might be undertaken by a much smaller organization.

Another feature of very great importance at this time was the improvement in the cooperation between the different groups working in Palestine. Previous excavations had been in charge of men from a number of different nations, some of which hated each other. Even groups from the same nation were sometimes very jealous of one another. The American School of Oriental Research did much to promote the development of a spirit of cooperation among the different groups. Much credit is due here to Dr. William Foxwell Albright, who was director of the American School of Oriental Research at Jerusalem from 1921 to 1929. Professor Albright gained the confidence of most of the various groups engaged in Palestinian excavation. They knew that they could trust him not to publish anything he learned from their excavations until they had published it first. Consequently they received him at their excavations, showed him what they were doing, gave him the opportunity of learning from the discoveries that they had made, and, in turn, profited from the increased understanding that he gained from his own study and from his visits to many different sites. The general spirit of cooperation that was developed in Palestine during this time did much to increase the results attained by all the various groups.

Only one important figure refused to cooperate. That was Sir William Flinders Petrie, who came to Palestine in 1927 after a lifetime of work in Egypt. Petrie had been a great pioneer in Egyptian excavation, and as a matter of principle had to reach his own conclusions without being affected by the ideas of others. The result was that, while generally friendly with other excavators, he did not allow himself to be influenced by their ideas or discoveries. In his previous brief visit to Palestine, more than 30 years earlier, Petrie had laid the foundation upon which all work in Palestine was now done, but most excavators continued from this foundation along quite different lines from those he himself now followed.

The great amount of work done after 1919 was far better than the much smaller amount that had preceded because much had been learned in the process of excavation, techniques were greatly improved, and the results were available to all the different groups.

Another advantage came from the fact that during these years three very large excavations were carried on in Palestine. Each of these took an extremely large mound and went to work with great care, starting from the top

36

and examining everything on the mound. Such excavations sometimes fail to yield as much of sensational interest as is occasionally produced by smaller ones, but the great amount of material gathered, and the progress that can be made through observation of the precise relationship of different types of material to each other, gives a background of information — particularly if the material is well published — that increases the effectiveness of all subsequent excavation.

A final cause of progress during these years was the presence in Palestine of experts who were there continuously, not merely there for a few weeks of excavation. Among these should be mentioned Dr. William F. Albright, already alluded to above, and Dr. Clarence Fisher, an expert in the techniques of excavation, who personally began two of the great expeditions of this period.

2. The Great Expeditions

The first of the three great expeditions was the excavation of Beth-shan, which was begun in 1921 and continued for many years. Beth-shan was a very large city, occupying a strategic place since it controlled the pass between the Valley of Jezreel and the Jordan Valley. In NT times the Hellenistic city at this place was called Scythopolis. While material was found here from many periods, the most interesting was from the Canaanite time. Four different Canaanite temples were excavated. It would seem that the Egyptians held the city as a fortress for many years and three stone monuments with large inscriptions in Egyptian hieroglyphics were found. Later on, the city was occupied by a Philistine garrison and it was here that they hung the bodies of Saul and Jonathan on the wall (I Sam. 31: 10-12).

The second of the great excavations, that of Megiddo, threw more light on the time of Israelite settlement. Megiddo had an equally strategic position guarding a vital pass between the coastal plain and the inner valleys. It was necessary that any army going in either direction between Mesopotamia and Egypt, or between Asia Minor and Egypt, should pass near Megiddo. Many strategic battles have been fought there and the name, which in the Hebrew is *har Megiddo*, or "hill of Megiddo," is mentioned in the NT as Armageddon (Rev. 16:16). It was here that King Josiah was killed when he tried to stop an Egyptian army from going up to mix in the stirring events accompanying the death throes of the Assyrian Empire (II Kings 23:29-30; II Chron. 35: 20-24).

A start had been made in excavating Megiddo as early as 1903, when the German Palestine Society began to conduct excavations there. A number of interesting things were found, but the results were not what they might have been because of the unfortunate necessity of using the unsatisfactory trench system of excavation.

In 1925 the University of Chicago began a long period of excavations here with Dr. Fisher as the first director. The results threw important light on many interesting matters both in the Israelite and in the Canaanite period. In the Early Bronze age Megiddo was surrounded by a massive city wall, originally 13 feet thick and later strengthened to twice that thickness. Very interesting carved ivories were found from the times when great Egyptian armies marched through this region. To the Bible student the most interesting discovery made at Megiddo was the great stables of King Solomon, which we shall discuss later (V.E.2).

The third of the great expeditions was a new attempt to uncover the remains of the city of Lachish. Lachish was the second most important city in Judah. When King Sennacherib was unable to conquer Jerusalem, he consoled himself with a great bas-relief put up in his palace to commemorate his capture of Lachish. In 1890 it had been the desire of the Palestine Exploration Fund that Petrie excavate Lachish, and the work that he and his successors did at Tell el-Hesy was described as late as 1930 as "the Lachish Expedition." However, doubts were raised as to whether this actually was Lachish, and in 1933 a well-financed British Expedition began work at Tell ed-Duweir, a larger mound somewhat farther E, and continued to excavate for a number of years. As in the other two great expeditions, a tremendous amount of detailed material was unearthed, throwing light upon many facets of the culture of Canaanite and Israelite civilizations. Most interesting from the viewpoint of Biblical archaeology was the discovery of a large number of inscriptions written on pieces of potsherd during the time of the final Babylonian attack on Lachish. These writings are frustrating because of the briefness of their reference to contemporary events. Many exact connections with the Bible have been imagined, but it is difficult to prove any of them conclusively. However, the general information that can be gleaned from them about Hebrew language and writing, and about the general situation of the time, is most useful.

3. Excavations of the American School of Oriental Research

We have already noticed the great part that the American School of Oriental Research played in encouraging cooperation among the different groups active in Palestine. However, the School itself also had an active part in the work of excavation.

Its first effort was a small but interesting work conducted in 1922 by Dr. William F. Albright at Tell el-Ful, a mound located a few miles N of Jerusalem. According to an old tradition, it covers the site of Gibeah of Benjamin, the place where Saul had his capital. In the excavation no writing was found that would prove the identity of the town. Indications point to the accuracy of the identification, but without precise confirmation it cannot be considered as completely established. For a small excavation the amount of definite information gained was surprisingly great.

Every second year between 1926 and 1932 the American Schools cooperated with President M. G. Kyle of Xenia Theological Seminary in the Excavation of Tell Beit Mirsim, 13 miles SW of Hebron. Very extensive work was done in uncovering this town, which its excavators believe to be the site of Kirjath-sepher, later Debir (cf. Joshua 15: 15-16; Judges 1:11-12). Here again, despite the name of the city ("Town of the Book" or, as Dr. Albright suggests, "Town of the Scribe"), little writing was found and no conclusive proof could be given of the identification, though the situation fits the Biblical references so well that it would seem extremely likely that it is correct. Light was thrown on Canaanite and Israelite culture at many points.

In 1931 the American School cooperated in a one-season excavation at Beth-zur, a little to the N of Hebron (Joshua 15:58; II Chron. 11:7; Neh. 3:16). This was the site of one of the fiercely fought struggles in the Maccabean revolt (*I Macc.* 4:28-35).

In 1937-9 the American School at Jerusalem, under the directorship of Dr. Nelson Glueck, conducted a very interesting excavation at the N end of the Gulf of Aqaba, at what is probably the site of the ancient city of Eziongeber. This is where Solomon built his seaport for trade with Ophir (I Kings 9:26). The excavation showed the tremendous power of the Jerusalem ruler who could build such a city so far from his headquarters.

4. Other Excavations

In this brief summary, it will be possible to mention only some of the most important excavations that took place in this extremely important period of Palestinian work.

First we shall mention the Harvard Excavations at Samaria, which had already been carried on for three seasons, between 1908 and 1910, at the site of ancient Samaria. The last two of these were under the direction of G. A. Reisner, who had done outstanding work in excavation in Egypt. The work was a model of technical excellence. It showed that Samaria had been built by Omri as stated in the Bible (I Kings 16:24). Palaces of Omri, of Ahab, and of Jeroboam II were uncovered. These excavations were continued in 1931 and following years. For a time, Samaria was a larger and more prominent capital than Jerusalem.

Extremely interesting work has been done at Jericho, where excavation was carried out by the German Orient Society from 1907 to 1909. It was continued by Professor John Garstang in 1930-36, and has now been carried further by Miss K. M. Kenyon of the British School of Archaeology in Jerusalem, who dug here in 1952 and succeeding years. For a comparatively small mound this is a tremendous amount of work. Jericho occupies a vital strategic location and was the scene of one of the most dramatic events in Biblical history (Josh. 6).

There has been great interest in everything that is found there and much argument about many features of it. In a place as important to history as this, it is all too easy to elaborate theories often built on silence and to allow these theories to get wide publicity, even though later their subsequent correction or change may reach but a small fraction of those who heard the original theory.

Many other expeditions of medium or small importance were carried on between the wars, and important light on various aspects of Palestinian culture was derived from each of them.

D. Palestinian Archaeology Since the Second World War

The Palestinian discovery that has attracted more attention than any other since the Second World War was the finding of the Dead Sea Scrolls. Since their primary interest concerns theories of derivation in relation to the NT rather than to the OT, discussion of them will be left to sections VI.B, and VI.F.

A great deal of other excavation has been carried on in Palestine during the past 20 years, though work has been hampered by the splitting of Palestine in 1948 into two parts, with a no-man's land between them. The riots, upheavals, and fighting accompanying the partition naturally disrupted archaeological work to a great extent. As a result of the partition, the most fruitful and fertile sections of Palestine now belong to the state of Israel. However, a great part of this area was possessed by the Philistines in Biblical times. Perhaps eighty per cent of the places where important events in ancient Israel took place are in the state of Jordan, held by the Arabs. Thus the overwhelming bulk of the important archaelogical sites are not now accessible to the Jews.

In Jordan a considerable amount of excavation has been carried on. The work of J. P. Free at Dothan during a number of years, of J. B. Pritchard at Gibeon, of G. E. Wright at Shechem, and other excavations have added much detail to our knowledge of the culture of ancient Palestine. As mentioned above, work at Jericho was continued during this period. Work at Beth-zur was resumed in 1957.

In Israel interest in archaeology has been great. A Department of Antiquities is very active. Whenever any public or private construction unearths something of archaeological interest anywhere in the land, work has to stop immediately until experts can come and determine whether it is necessary to make a thorough investigation before other activities are allowed to proceed. The most important ancient place in the land of Israel is probably Hazor, the town from which Sisera came to fight against Barak. Under the able direction of Yigael Yadin, Israelite archaeologists have carried on a number of seasons of excavation at Hazor, beginning in 1955, and have found much that throws interesting light on details of ancient Canaanite life.

One can never know when an expedition in either Israel or Jordan may find something with dramatic impact upon Biblical study, such as the earlier discovery of Solomon's stables or Solomon's seaport. In recent years most of the excavation is giving helpful information on particular details and has not yielded such great steps forward. One never knows, however, when something of this type may occur.

E. Relation of Palestinian Archaeology to the Bible

1. The Situation in General

Before considering specific relations of Palestinian archaeology to the Bible, it is necessary to look briefly at the relation of each of these to history and culture.

First, we note that it is not the purpose of the Bible to give us a complete history of ancient Palestine. Its purpose is rather to show how man has turned away from God, and how God has provided for man a marvelous plan of redemption. The history of Palestine is important in this connection but is far from being the real objective of the Biblical writing. The periods or activities that are vital from a religious viewpoint are stressed and clearly explained in the Bible, and only so much of the political and cultural background as is necessary for their understanding. Events of great political or cultural importance are sometimes completely passed over in the Bible because they are not related to its purpose. The Bible tells us much about the history of Palestine, but there are great gaps in its coverage of this subject, and many matters are left unexplained.

The situation is somewhat similar when we look at the relation of Palestinian archaeology to history. We have seen that very little written material from OT times has been discovered in Palestine. Nothing has been found there in the way of a connected account of contemporary events, or of a presentation of an Israelite king's claim to have done mighty deeds. Practically all the findings consist of material objects. It would be very difficult to interpret these historically if it were not for the fact that many of them have similarities to things that have been found in Egypt and in Mesopotamia, and that occasionally we find datable objects from those lands. We have noticed that pottery enables us to tell approximately how long and in what period a certain town was occupied. This, however, does not give us certainty about the name of the

town unless we find written matter that contains the name. It would be impossible to construct a coherent history of ancient Palestine simply from the archaeological material. Having evidence from other sources, the archaeological material fits in with it at many points and adds a good deal to the general picture.

Thus it is even more true of Palestinian archaeology than of the Bible, that what we can learn from it about the political and cultural history of Palestine, while important, is very incomplete. Consequently, most of our relationships in this section will fall under the head of general corroboration rather than of special corroboration. Without written material it is very difficult to get much that properly belongs under the head of special corroboration.

2. General Corroboration

The general picture of life in Palestine that is presented in the Bible and the picture that can be gained from archaeology fit together remarkably well. Let us briefly survey the history and notice some of the evidences that have come to light.

Excavators in Palestine have shown great interest in the earliest levels of cities that existed before the invention of writing. While much of real importance for prehistory may eventually be learned from Palestine, this belongs only to a very slight extent to the field of Biblical archaeology, since the first contact of the Biblical narrative with Palestine occurs at the coming of Abraham.

The Biblical account of the patriarchs has many points of contact with Palestinian archaeology. The Bible shows Abraham coming into Palestine and there moving back and forth with his flocks and herds over a restricted area, staying a few weeks or months in one place and then moving to another, coming back to the same areas from time to time as he moved N and S through the land. Abraham's movements were mostly restricted to the central N and S ridge, often designated as the hill country, and he rarely spent much time E or W of that general area. In modern Palestine it would be hard to think of someone as carrying on this type of life in the hill country since that is where so many of the towns are, as was also the case in the period of Israelite occupation. Archaeological evidence shows that at the time of Abraham the greater amount of settlement was down in the valley, and the extensive pasture land in the hill country was fairly open, so that it was possible for groups to move freely back and forth from N to S, as the patriarchs are pictured doing. These stories could not possibly have been invented in the time of the Israelite kingdom, as many critics hold, for no one would then have imagined a situation so different from the one that he saw before him.

This situation is vividly illustrated in the story of the separation of Abraham and Lot. Gen. 13 tells us that when Abram came back from Egypt, having amassed a great amount of wealth there, he pitched his tent between Bethel and Ai (v. 3). Lot also had great numbers of flocks and herds, and the region did not have enough conveniently located pasture for both men to be able to utilize it properly. This naturally led to strife between the herdsmen of Abram's cattle and the herdsmen of Lot's cattle, as to which of them would have prior use of the nearer pasture land, and so produced a real danger because of the presence of hostile people in the area (v. 7). In this situation Abram suggested to Lot that the two should go separate ways, and he offered to let Lot make his choice of areas. Then we read in verse 10, "And Lot lifted up his eyes and beheld all the plain of Jordan, that it was well-watered everywhere, before the Lord destroyed Sodom and Gomorrah, even as the Garden of the Lord, like the land of Egypt, as thou comest unto Zoar." Lot chose this plain of Jordan, leaving Abram in the hill country. To anyone visiting Palestine today this story would be quite fantastic. The hill country in the region of Bethel and Ai has many small towns and much excellent pasture land, while the region of the Jordan Valley is mostly barren wilderness. Lot's choice would be inconceivable today. The same situation existed in the time of the later Israelite kingdom, or in fact almost any time after Joshua's day. Eduard Meyer, the noted German historian, contrasted the Jordan Valley with the Nile Valley in 1928 in the following words: "Absolutely barren lay also the Jordan Valley south of Beth-shan and Pella, burning hot between the mountain walls on both sides, through which it cut its broad and deep way. . . . Here the attempt was never made to utilize the soil and to make it productive by systematic irrigation, as was done in the Nile Valley under essentially the same conditions."

It is only in the present century that new evidence has come to light. In 1926 an American expedition into the Jordan Valley found a number of previously unrecognized tells, on which the pottery showed that there had been occupation about the time of Abraham and none since. In the following years many more were found. The only way that all these towns in the Jordan Valley could have supported themselves would have been by utilizing the water of the Jordan River for irrigation. When this was done, the fertile land would produce great crops. It would seem that after the destruction of Sodom and Gomorrah many of the irrigation ditches were left untended and became stagnant pools, fertile sources of malaria, so that the depopulation produced by the destruction of Sodom and Gomorrah was increased by the effects of malaria. By the time of Joshua, Jericho was the only town of any importance remaining in the Jordan Valley, which in Abraham's time had been a very prosperous and well-occupied area, exactly as described in Gen. 13. It is extremely improbable that anyone in the time of the Israelite kingdom would invent a story that described conditions so very different from those that had already existed for hundreds of years.

Gen. 19 gives a terrible picture of the corruption of Sodom, with great riots. The mob threatened to do harm to the guests of Lot, and the only way that Lot himself escaped was that an angel pulled him into the door of his house. In Gen. 15:16 Abraham was told that "the iniquity of the Amorites is not yet full," and that consequently the divinely-ordered destruction would not take place for yet a period of time. Excavation of the pre-Israelite period in various Palestinian sites has given evidence of a civilization of high culture and wealth, but of constantly increasing corruption, that reached, shortly before the Israelite conquest, a state of moral degradation scarcely to be paralleled elsewhere. Excavation at Tell Beit Mirsim has shown that in the Canaanite time it was a very prosperous community. In the early days of Israelite settlement, everything was far simpler and economically on a lower level. In the later Israelite time, culture and wealth reached a position fully equal to that of the Canaanite period. However, a sharp difference between the high point of Israelite prosperity and that of the Canaanites is evidenced by the difference in the nature of the doors. In the Canaanite time each house had a very strong doorpost, so that it could resist a riot similar to that which Lot faced in Sodom. The house of the later Israelite time had only a little hanging over the door, giving mute evidence of the comparative security of the later Israelite period, as compared with the degeneracy of the latter part of the Canaanite period.

All over Palestine there is evidence of a sharp break between Canaanite and Israelite occupation, often marked by a thick layer of ashes separating the two different cultures. Similar evidence is found at the end of the Israelite monarchy. The Bible tells us that they were conquered by invaders from distant Mesopotamia and the bulk of the people taken into exile. The excavations show cities at a high stage of culture, coming to a sudden end, with a destruction followed by a long period in which there is no evidence of any extensive occupation in the land. The Lachish letters vividly illustrate the situation at the time of the great Babylonian invasion just before the downfall of the Judean kingdom.

Sometimes great doubt has been expressed as to the reality of the high point in Israelite prosperity and culture, described in the Bible as having occurred at the time of Solomon. H. G. Wells stated that the alleged greatness of Solomon was badly overestimated. He said that actually Solomon was a petty kinglet, not at all of the calibre that the Bible would make one believe. However, in 1928 Dr. P. O. O. Guy, who was Director of the excavation at Megiddo from 1927 to 1933, found that in the fourth stratum from the top, which he attributed to the time of Solomon, a large part of this great city was given over to stalls for horses, illustrating the statement of I Kings 9:15-19 that among the cities Solomon rebuilt, one of which is designated as Megiddo, were whole cities for his chariots and for his horsemen. Only a ruler of great power and wealth could have established this extensive layout at Megiddo.

A few of the later archaeologists have preferred to attribute to the time of Ahab the particular stalls that Guy found, but archaeologists are by no means agreed on this.

Further evidence of the power and wisdom of King Solomon came to light as the result of Glueck's excavations at Ezion-geber in 1937 to 1940, which showed that this town at the N end of the Gulf of Aqaba, far S of the Dead Sea, had been built at the time of Solomon in accordance with a definite master plan, by people who gave evidence of Israelite culture rather than that of the surrounding region.

The statement in I Kings 9:26-28 that Solomon built a navy of ships at Ezion-geber to trade with the regions to the south had been previously much doubted because there was no apparent reason to build it at that location, so far overland from Jerusalem. If the purpose had been to export the excellent textiles produced in Judah at the time, it would have been far more economical to have them carried down to Suez and then, after a short portage, to have gone down the other arm of the Red Sea to the region of Ophir. However, in Glueck's first expedition to Ezion-geber he had found remains of ancient copper mines from the time of Solomon a short distance N of the gulf, much too far south for economical transportation to Jerusalem, but near enough to the Gulf of Aqaba to make it feasible to use them for trade with Ophir. This satisfactorily explained why Solomon built Ezion-geber where he did, and also provided special corroboration of the oft-doubted statement in Deuteronomy 8:9 that Palestine is a land "out of whose hills thou mayest dig brass (Heb., copper)."

Up to 1966 Dr. Glueck had not yet published a full scientific account of the excavations at Ezion-geber, but at the time of the excavation and in the subsequent years he had frequently declared that the central feature of the city was an industrial structure, utilizing the wind from the N in such a way as to make it possible to smelt ore at a high temperature, thus applying the principle of the modern blast furnace. Building such a city so far from Jerusalem, according to one definite plan, shows an aggregation of great power and wealth. In addition, Glueck felt that the principles utilized illustrated the Biblical picture of the wisdom of Solomon and surpassed anything else known to us in the ancient world from that period.

Twenty years after these excavations Beno Rothenberg made extensive studies of copper mining in the regions N of the Dead Sea and criticized Glueck's results so intensively that Glueck himself retracted part of his previous view, and said that what he had formerly thought to be a smelter was probably a storehouse for grain. However, he still declared that there was evidence of copper smelting at Ezion-geber.

Details of the methods of smelting at Ezion-geber still remain in doubt, yet the new theories also involve serious difficulties.

Such problems illustrate the fact that Palestinian archaeology is a science that is moving forward, so that there is great flux and uncertainty in many of its features. This is also true, though to a lesser extent, of the archaeology of Egypt and Mesopotamia, where more written material has been found than in Palestine. On the part of many archaeologists there is a strong bias against complete acceptance of the accuracy of Scripture and this undoubtedly warps conclusions at certain places. Yet even if all the questioning of past assertions of Biblical accuracy could be proven, there would still remain a great amount of solidly established material strongly supporting the general dependability of the Scripture. It should be noted that none of the questions that have been raised about Megiddo or Ezion-geber involve doubt as to the accuracy of the Scripture; they merely question the complete dependability of certain evidences previously alleged in support of Biblical statements. Even if these particular evidences should be proven wrong, it would not prove the Biblical statements false; it would only remove certain corroborating evidences that had previously been considered well established.

Palestinian archaeology is constantly bringing new instances of general corroboration of Biblical history.

3. Special Corroboration

Instances of special corroboration are not so many from Palestine as from Mesopotamia, yet there is a substantial number, one of which was mentioned at the end of the last section. The Book of Genesis names quite a number of cities as having been occupied in the time of Abraham or his immediate descendants. Many a town mentioned only in later books has, on examination, proved to have been founded at a later period, but every Palestinian city named in Genesis with one exception, has been shown to have been in existence at the time of the Patriarchs. This one exception, Hebron, is in a valley with four streams, at a place so ideally suited for human occupation that it would be strange if there were not a town there in Abraham's time, though its precise location has not yet been found.

The location of cities named in the Bible is a particular type of special corroboration. There is always the problem of determining just what town is buried in a certain tell. Various tests

must be applied: the question whether the name has been preserved; the question of its relationship to particular events described in the Bible as having occurred at or near it; and its relationship to other places mentioned in connection with it, as in the account of a journey, or the description of tribal borders. One must also consider the question of whether it was occupied at the periods at which the Bible says it was, and whether it is a large enough place to fit the requirements of the Biblical references. When these tests are applied, the identity of many places in Palestine can be considered as very certain. In the case of others the degree of probability may be great, but there may still be considerable uncertainty. Usually for absolute certainty some bit of written material is highly desirable. Examination of various cities to see just when they were occupied, and comparison with the Biblical references to them, provides many interesting points of special corroboration.

An interesting instance of special corroboration from Palestine came from the excavation of Beth-zur in 1931. It involves the references to gold drachmas in Ezra 2:69 and Neh. 7:70,71. The Hebrew word דַּרְכְּמוֹנִים fits exactly with the form used in inscriptions by Phoenician sailors at the Piraeus, the harbor of Athens, when referring to the Attic drachma. The translators of the AV rendered the word as "dram," an English measure, which is derived from the Greek word *drachma*. Yet since the Hebrew uses the word drachma it would seem reasonable to translate it "drachma," if this is what is actually meant. It used to be thought extremely unlikely that in the Persian period in Palestine such a standard as the Attic drachma would be used. The ARV of 1901 renders the word as "daric," which was the name of a coin made by the Persians, named after the Persian king Darius. This might seem to be a more natural interpretation, but it is not the word that the Hebrew actually uses. At Beth-zur, in a level belonging to the Persian Period, a group of coins was found that included several good examples of coins made in Palestine in imitation of the Greek drachma, showing that the Hebrew word can safely be taken exactly as it stands.

4. Help in Interpretation

Any increase in knowledge of the geographical and cultural background of Palestine is bound to make more understandable the historical and cultural statements of the OT, and this is true of some of the material discussed above under general or special corroboration. One additional instance where this background was formerly completely misunderstood will be mentioned here. In I Samuel we find a number of Philistines holding a much larger number of Israelites in subjection because the Philistines had access to sources of iron and knowledge of how to work it. This gave them a great advantage over the Israelites, who had not yet entered the Iron Age. I Sam. 13:19-22 indicates that only Saul and Jonathan were able to secure iron weapons, and therefore the Israelites were at a great disadvantage against the better-armed Philistines. However, it does state that the Israelites were able to secure iron agricultural implements. (In some of the excavations iron agricultural implements have begun to appear at a somewhat earlier time than iron weapons.) However, one statement in the English translation seemed very strange. After reading in v. 20 that the Israelites went down to the Philistines to sharpen their implements, we read in v. 21: "yet they had a file for the mattocks, (etc.)." If they

had a file for all these implements why would they go down to the Philistines to get them sharpened? Although it seems quite confusing, the translators of the AV can hardly be blamed, since the Hebrew word *pim*, which they translate "file," occurs only once in the entire OT, and they had no way of knowing its real meaning. Now at several places excavations have brought to light small weights marked *pym*, thus bearing the same consonants as the word used in I Sam. 13:21. Since it applies to a weight, it is easy to see that it should be vocalized not as pim but as *payim*, and thus means two-thirds of a shekel, which is exactly what each of these weights has been found to weigh. So it becomes clear that the intention of the verse is to point out the high price that the Israelites had to pay to get their tools sharpened. Thus the cultural situation becomes understandable in view of the material excavated, which, in turn, corroborates the general situation described in the Biblical passage.

5. Derivation

In the past, books were written to show that the Israelites derived most of their religious and ethical ideas from the Canaanites. In view of the small amount of written material from Palestinian excavation, there is very little evidence in Palestinian archaeology for or against these statements; yet the great difference in culture, and especially in moral standards, shown by the excavations, would speak against it. However, as mentioned above (IV.A.) the Ugaritic literature found at Ras Shamra in Syria gives a basis for comparison of Canaanite religious ideas with those of the Bible. This literature is very helpful for interpretation of certain Biblical references to heathen religion, but shows clearly that Biblical religion was quite distinct from that of the Canaanites and that the stories about the Canaanite gods find no parallel in the Biblical story.

6. The Problem of the Date Of the Conquest

A few years ago there were scholars who denied that there had ever been an extensive Israelite conquest of Palestine. Instead, they insisted that small groups of ancestors of the later Israelites had drifted in from the desert so that the population had gradually changed from Canaanite to Israelite. Today it is questionable if anyone would hold such a position. Too many cities have been excavated and shown to have had tremendous, powerful walls at the end of the Canaanite period. Often a thick burnt layer separates the Canaanite remains from those of Israelite civilization above. The fact of an Israelite conquest can today hardly be doubted.

However, the date of the conquest still remains a question. This is, of course, closely connected with the question of the date of the Exodus from Egypt (cf. II.E.5). The figure given in 1 Kings 6:1 seems to many to decide the matter conclusively in favor of an Exodus during the 18th dynasty in Egypt, and therefore a Conquest about 40 years later. Some students would even feel that Biblical integrity was dependent upon the acceptance of this particular date for the Exodus and the Conquest.

The present writer does not feel this way. Systems of chronology such as we have today, of numbering centuries one after the other, were hardly in existence until well along in the Christian era. The Bible does not tell us the month in which Abraham left Ur, nor the month in which David died. God could have caused this information and thousands of similar facts to be included in the Bible if He had chosen. The Bible does not tell us in what century the Exodus occurred. If we can determine these matters from other evidence, they are interesting to know, but they should never be considered as articles of faith.

For many years there have been those who would place the Exodus from Egypt about two centuries later. This has usually been based upon the mention of the city of Ramses in Ex. 1:11. This name came into prominence in the 19th dynasty, and it is unlikely that it would have been made the name of an important city previous to that time. For many years it was considered almost a settled matter that Ramses II was the pharaoh of the oppression, and Merneptah the pharaoh of the Exodus. Again it must be said that we cannot be certain. The Bible has simply not given us the data on which to be sure of the date of the Exodus.

When we look at the evidence from Palestine, it again is inconclusive. While the book of Joshua tells us of a thorough-going conquest with most of the cities completely overcome, there are statements in Joshua and a still greater number in Judges which suggest that after the first great conquest there was still much land to be taken. In the case of many cities whose armies had been defeated and their king destroyed, people might have been able to return to the city and to re-establish themselves so well that considerable time elapsed before they were again conquered. This is very definitely true of Jerusalem, whose king was overcome by Joshua (Josh. 10:1-27; 12:7,10) but which was a pagan city in the midst of the land (cf. Judges 19:10-12) until its final conquest by David (II Sam. 5:6,7).

The arguments as to an early or late

date of the Exodus often seem to be given in the manner of a lawyer determined to prove a particular point, rather than of a researcher seeking for light in order to determine something that is not yet known. Some new discovery may make the matter absolutely final, but up to the present it must be considered a question on which we do not yet have sufficient light.

7. General Conclusions Regarding OT Archaeology

Palestinian archaeology, like that of Egypt and Mesopotamia, has done much to show the accuracy of individual Biblical statements and has done much more to show the general accuracy of the historical background. As a result, even unbelieving scholars tend more and more to accept the Bible as a prime historical source for the reconstruction of ancient history. No evidence from archaeology has proven any Biblical statement to be false. Occasionally, as in the case of the former attitude toward the presence of camels in Egypt, or toward the existence of King Belshazzar of Babylon, evidence in hand is utilized by anti-Biblical scholars to try to show that the Bible is inaccurate on a particular point. Many such problems have disappeared in the light of advancing knowledge, and it is safe to say that all of them will be ironed out as more is learned about the history and culture of ancient times. Many a problem in OT interpretation that seemed very puzzling at the beginning of this century has been solved by archaeological evidence, and we can confidently recognize that the book that God has inspired and kept from error for the presentation to us of vital spiritual and ethical truths is equally dependable whenever it touches upon material facts of history or of culture.

A. Comparison with the Archaeology of Palestine In OT Times

The principles that we have already observed in connection with Palestinian archaeology are just as valid for the NT period. We meet the same difficulty here.

VI. Palestine in NT Times Most of the written material has disappeared because the convenient writing material that was easily available was not durable. Very little material actually written in NT times has been preserved. Aside from the Dead Sea Scrolls, which will be discussed later, practically all our written material that has been found from the time of the events described in the NT consists of brief inscriptions on ossuaries. An ossuary is a limestone casket in which the bones of a deceased person were collected after the flesh had decomposed. Hundreds of these have been found in the Jerusalem area in tombs of people buried during the last century before the city was destroyed in A.D. 70. These ossuaries have on them short inscriptions in Greek or Aramaic, which, though very brief, have considerable historical value for students of the NT.

There are certain differences between the archeology of Palestine as it relates to the NT and as it relates to the OT. The NT is not directly concerned with great political events. Christianity began inconspicuously. The Son of Man had no place to lay his head. To the external eye he appeared to be merely a Galilean peasant. He went about with comparatively simple people. There was nothing here that would lead a contemporary ruler to put up a stone monument or to make a bas-relief on the wall of his palace. Moreover, the NT period is comparatively so short that we cannot expect a great deal of light from archaeology. Many periods of OT history have very little archaeological evidence to throw light upon them. Other periods have contacts with great political events that left imposing archaeological monuments. While OT history extends over a thousand years, the entire history described in the NT occupies little more than half a century. Another difficulty with NT archaeology is that the most terrible upheaval in the whole history of Palestine took place just after the end of the NT period. Jesus had told the disciples that the temple would be destroyed, so that not one stone would be left upon another. The devastation in connection with the Roman conquest was very far-reaching. These changes so soon after the NT events made a very sweeping change in the condition of the country as a whole, and particularly in the Jerusalem area. This was followed 60 years later by the rebellion of Bar Cochba, with further turmoil and destruction, followed by banishment of all Jews from the area. Later on, the Arab conquest made still further changes. Very soon the external appearance of the land was very different in many regards from what it had been in NT times.

Another difference between NT and OT times in Palestine is that we are not nearly so dependent upon archaeology for illuminating material relating to what is contained in the sacred text. Before the rise of modern archaeology, we knew practically nothing about life in OT times except for the statements in the OT itself. Classical Greek writings mostly dealt with events after the end of the OT. In the case of the NT, the writings of Josephus contain extensive descriptions of life and historical events in Palestine, and there are a few references to Palestine in the writings of pagan historians. These materials give us far more with which to check the accuracy and integrity of the NT docu-

ments than we can expect to secure from archaeology. They are drawn on extensively in the discussion of these various subjects in other articles in this encyclopedia.

One great field of interest for students of the NT is to know where various events occurred. Archaeology can help in throwing light on the location of places mentioned in the NT. Unfortunately, quite a few of the events in the NT, such as the Sermon on the Mount, occurred at places that are not specifically named, and archaeology can do nothing to prove where they occurred. Jerusalem of the time of Christ is buried under debris and later occupation is above it. The present city (or rather two cities) has spread out over a wide area. Extensive excavation within the city is very difficult. However, investigation of neighboring places such as Bethany, or particular areas in Jerusalem, like the Tower of Antonia, is possible. Also, searching for a definite objective, such as the location of the various walls of ancient Jerusalem, can often be carried on with very good results. Herodian Jericho, about a mile from OT Jericho, was excavated in 1950-51. Herod erected the Jerusalem temple in strict accord with Hebrew specifications, but at Jericho he built a sumptuous palace that is like a bit of first-century Rome, transported to Palestine.

B. The Discovery of The Dead Sea Scrolls

Undoubtedly the most important discovery that has ever been made in relation to NT times, and also the most unexpected, was the discovery of the Dead Sea Scrolls. In 1947 a Bedouin shepherd came by accident upon some leather scrolls wrapped in jars and hidden in a cave. Eventually, half of the group of scrolls that he found came into the possession of the Hebrew University at Jerusalem, and the other half into the possession of the Syrian archbishop. Later the archbishop's scrolls were purchased by the Jews, so that the whole set of material from Cave One is now in Jewish hands.

For a time heated discussion was waged about the date when these scrolls were written. Most scholars are convinced that it has now been conclusively demonstrated that all of the Qumran scrolls were written during the two or three centuries preceding the destruction of Jerusalem in A.D. 70.

The first discovery included the only complete Bible book of any length that had yet been found from so early a date. This was a complete copy of Isaiah, rather carelessly written, but preserving a text that is almost identical with the text of Isaiah in our present Hebrew Bible, though nearly a thousand years earlier than the earliest copy available before this discovery. Numerous portions of another copy of Isaiah were also included in this group of scrolls. Later search in other caves has brought many more Bible portions to light, including a great many small fragments. Within a few years parts of almost every OT book had been found. These may eventually prove to be of great help for textual criticism of the OT, and thus be very valuable for OT studies.

The makers of the scrolls belonged to a previously unknown Jewish sect. They are generally called Essenes, since this is a term used by Josephus and Pliny to describe groups of Jews who went out into the wilderness and lived an ascetic life there. However, some of the characteristics of the Essenes as given by these ancient writers differ from those of the group at Khirbet Qumran, the community headquarters where the scrolls were made. Khirbet Qumran was excavated in 1951-66. One of its rooms proved to be a Scriptorium, with a table and inkwells, and everything set out for the copying of manuscripts.

Nearly half of the scrolls are copies of OT books. Quite a number are commentaries on portions of the OT, interpreted by the particular ideas of the sect and showing their outlook on life and their theology. A few of the scrolls contain rules for the life of the community. There has been much discussion of the relation of this material to Christianity, which we shall examine below, under Derivation.

C. General Corroboration

The NT assumes a situation in which a foreign group, the Romans, is holding the Jewish people in subjection, with the Jews divided into various groups, such as the Sadducees and the Pharisees, all of them longing for freedom from Roman oppression. These and other features of the situation in Palestine are already well corroborated from the writings of Josephus and from other sources.

D. Special Corroboration

Here again we do not have as much material from Biblical archaeology as we would like. Far more is to be found in the writings of Josephus than in any archaeological material yet available from this period. However, some very interesting points have come to light at which archaeological evidence answers objections that have been made to the dependability of the NT narratives. The term Rabbi, rendered *didaskolos*, "master" or "teacher," in Greek, is applied to Jesus at many points in the Gospel of John. Some Rabbinic scholars have insisted that this usage is an anachronism, common in the second century A.D., but never found in the first century. In 1930, when a first-century tomb near Jerusalem was excavated, there was found in it an ossuary

49

on which there was a Greek name, Theodotion, in Aramaic characters, together with the Greek word *didaskolos* as title of the man who bore this name.

There have been scholars who asserted that the personal names employed in the Gospels, especially in John, were fictitious and were chosen because of their meaning: "Mary," "Martha," "Elisabeth," "Salome," "Sapphira," and so on. The Gospels contain the name "Lazarus," an abbreviated form of "Eleazer." This abbreviated form is quite common on the ossuaries. "Jesus" and "Joseph" are commonly found. It is not at all strange that one ossuary contained the name of a "Jesus son of Joseph," perhaps one of the most ordinary combinations of the time. However, when this was found, there were those who seized upon it as proof that Jesus had not been raised from the dead but that these were actually the bones of the founder of the Christian religion. Aside from such unfortunate sensationalism, the finding of these various names is an interesting special corroboration of the background of the events in the Gospels.

An interesting instance of special corroboration relates to John 19:13, where we read that Pilate had Jesus brought to him at "a place that is called the Pavement, but in the Hebrew, Gabbatha." This is a rather peculiar expression. There was nothing exactly parallel to it in any other ancient material known to us. It has now been found that the Tower of Antonia had in its court a magnificent Roman pavement, about 2,500 square yards in area; so the term used by John, even though not otherwise corroborated by ancient material that has come down to us, is shown by archaeology to apply very naturally. Some of the names of the various governors and other officials mentioned in the Gospels or in the part

of the Book of Acts that relates to Palestine are known to us from Josephus. Very little has yet been found in the way of new archaeological discoveries corroborating these names, but there is always the possibility of further interesting discoveries.

E. Interpretation

Archaeology is of particular interest in relation to the NT for general orientation, for knowledge of the geographic background, and for understanding of the unusual customs of the time. We can also learn much about all these matters from Josephus.

Great interest attached to the identification of places at which particular events occurred. Many of the names mentioned in the NT are well known. In the case of others there can be considerable discussion as to their location. There must have been a great many synagogues in Palestine in the time of Christ, but the Romans would seem to have destroyed every one of them. The synagogue at Capernaum was formerly thought to be the one that the centurion built for the Jews (Luke 7:5). However, it now appears certain that this synagogue comes from the second century A.D. It may have been built on the model of the previous one, though this cannot be proven.

An interesting argument has been carried on for many years about the location of Calvary and the tomb of Christ. When Constantine's mother visited Jerusalem early in the fourth century, she found locations at which she believed these events to have occurred. Constantine ordered a beautiful church erected, with walls that would surround both places. Despite vicissitudes of earthquake, fire, and damage by invaders, the location that Helena selected has been remembered ever since. The church that now stands on the spot was built by the crusaders shortly after A.D. 1100. When Edward Robinson visited Jerusalem in 1838 he rejected the claims of this "Church of the Holy Sepulchre," since the NT states that the crucifixion occurred outside the city walls, and the Church of the Holy Sepulchre is inside the present walls of Jerusalem. However, the ardent defenders of the site insist that at the time of Christ the wall was further S than the present wall. Here archaeology might well play an important part in the determination of a point of Biblical geography. Unfortunately, the area S of the church is covered by a crowded city, so that excavation is virtually impossible. It may well be that we will never know with any certainty where the actual tomb of Christ was or where the crucifixion occurred. We know where Constantine thought it to be, but many upheavals had occurred during the previous three centuries, in which Christians showed little interest in preserving knowledge of sacred sites (cf. V.B). If the Lord had desired us to know the exact spot He could easily have caused more information on this point to be contained in the Gospel narrative.

About 1880 the famous General Charles G. Gordon adopted the view that the real Calvary was a hill, N of the present wall, which looks very much like a skull, and which has now come to be called "Gordon's Calvary." Near it is a rock-hewn tomb, now called "The Garden Tomb." Many people scoff at these identifications, declaring that there is no real ground for accepting them. Yet for help in interpretation more is gained from a place that graphically shows how the place originally appeared, even if it should not be the actual spot, than from one that looks altogether different, particularly since it also may or may not be the actual spot where the events occurred. At the Gar-

den Tomb one can see the city wall and the more distant Mount of Olives, much as they appeared at the time of Christ. One can look at Gordon's Calvary and see the marked resemblance to a skull. Perhaps this place did not look like a skull at that time, and some other did. In any event, we do not know the exact spot, but here we can vividly imagine the very situation in which the crucifixion occurred. In the Church of the Holy Sepulchre everything appears different from the way it did in the first century.

The NT speaks of "Decapolis" (Mt. 4:25; Mark 5:20; 7:31). This was a group of approximately ten Hellenistic cities in Palestine, most of them E of the Jordan River. At some of these cities, remains of Greek theaters and other Hellenistic buildings are visible today. One gets a feeling of the presence of the Greek culture in the midst of the land of Palestine. When we read how Jesus went across the Sea of Galilee, and how there the demons asked to be permitted to go into the swine (Mark 5:11-13; Luke 8:32-33), we might wonder how swine came to be in the land of the Jews, who were forbidden to eat pork. The answer is that this was the region of the Decapolis. Since these were pagan cities, it was quite natural to find swine in the area. Thus archaeology can help us to understand the local customs and the general geographical situation, and may at various points give us a better understanding of the meaning of particular words or particular situations.

F. Derivation

There have been many attempts to prove that Christianity is merely a development from some pagan cult or other ancient belief. None of these has been more effective in reaching a great number of people than the one that has based itself upon the Dead Sea Scrolls. An American journalist, Edmund Wilson, has written a romantic story of the finding of the scrolls and has proceeded to draw from the non-Biblical scrolls all sorts of utterly unwarranted conclusions, detrimental to Christianity, and these have been widely publicized. Wilson's book has been translated into many languages. In it he says: "The monastery of the Essenes, more than Bethlehem or Nazareth, is the cradle of Christianity." An English scholar, J. M. Allegro, has declared over the radio that Christian ideas about Christ were derived from the Qumran sect's ideas of their own teacher, who, he says, they thought of as "persecuted and crucified, and expected to rise again as priestly Messiah." A French scholar, Professor Dupont-Sommer, said that "the Galilean Teacher, as he is presented to us in the New Testament writings, appears in many respects as an astonishing reincarnation of the Teacher of Righteousness." A Swedish journalist has concluded as follows: "Christianity has come into existence in a completely natural way, as a Jewish sect. It is not necessary to believe in the miracle that God has interfered by a special act of mercy in order to save humanity."

These assertions rest upon the fact that the Qumran sect seems to have held in high esteem an individual whom they called "the Teacher of Righteousness." It is reasonable to think that he must have been a man of ability and energy, whose ideas found expression in the organization and continuance of the Qumran sect. But nowhere do we find an orderly account of his life and achievements. His name is never given, nor is there any clear indication of the time at which he lived. Many attempts have been made to identify him with some person known from other sources, but none of these can be proven.

Guesses as to his identity range over a period of two centuries. It has even been suggested that "the Teacher of Righteousness" represents a succession of men at the head of the sect rather than a particular individual who founded it.

The sweeping statements to which reference has been made suggest a belief that the story of Christ is really only a derivation from what the Qumran community thought about its "Teacher of Righteousness." This is a tremendous claim. Let us examine the facts.

In all the Qumran material that has yet been discovered and published, there is nowhere any statement that the Teacher of Righteousness was God, or that he claimed to be God, or that anyone else ever thought him to be God. There is no statement that he was born in a way different from any other mortals. There is no reference to his having been tempted by the devil. He made his followers take very strict ascetic vows, quite contrary to all that we find in the life of Jesus or in the attitude of the early church. There is no statement in the Qumran literature that he ever performed miracles of healing, and certainly no suggestion that he ever raised anyone from the dead. There is no evidence that he ever thought himself to be the Messiah. The Qumran sect seems to have expected that ultimately two Messiahs would come, a priestly Messiah and a kingly Messiah, but there is no proof that it expected that either of them would be the same person as the Teacher of Righteousness. There is no evidence that the Teacher of Righteousness ever said that he would return to earth on the clouds of heaven. There is no evidence that the Teacher ever said, or that anybody else ever thought, that there would be any special significance to his death. There is no real evidence that the Teacher of Righteousness was crucified. In fact it is not even stated, in any of the material that has come to light thus far, that he was put to death. There is no evidence that the Teacher of Righteousness was raised from the dead, or that anybody ever thought he had been raised from the dead, though there is reason to think that he may have been dead many years when the last of the scrolls was written. There is no evidence that the Qumran people ever thought that the Teacher of Righteousness could do something that would save an individual. Their only hope lay in following his teaching. Their faith was in what he had said, not, as in the case of Christianity, in him personally or in something he had done or could do. The followers of the Teacher of Righteousness formed a closed group, which no one could join without years of probation and the taking of very strict vows. This is entirely different from the procedure followed in the establishment of Christianity, as even a superficial glance at the Book of Acts will clearly show.

J. M. Allegro claims that the texts prove that the Teacher of Righteousness was crucified. However, this is purely an inference and, in the opinion of most scholars, an unjustified inference. Nowhere do the texts say that he was put to death, merely that he was "gathered in," a phrase which could just as well refer to death from natural causes. Even if Allegro's claim that the Teacher was crucified should eventually prove to be true, there is still no slightest evidence that he or anyone else attached any atoning significance to his death.

What a great number of differences between Christ and the Teacher of Rightcousness! None of the really distinctive points of Christianity are found in the beliefs of the Qumran sect!

It is true, of course, that some of the teachings of Jesus can be paralleled by statements in the scrolls. For that matter, many of them can be paralleled in the teachings of the Rabbis, preserved in the Talmud. Along with the similarities are also found very considerable differences. Such parallels may in some cases enable us to understand His meaning better, but they do not in any way detract from His claims about Himself. He was the Son of God, come down to die for our sins. Through faith in Him we can be saved. The beginning of Christianity was a miraculous interposition of God into human life, opening the way for lost humanity to find eternal life.

The Dead Sea Scrolls give remarkable evidence of the dependability of our OT text. They tell us some previously unknown facts about life in Palestine in the first century A.D. and before. But they neither add to nor detract from the unique achievements of the Son of God, who died that we might live.

A. The General Situation

The majority of the events described in the NT occurred in Palestine. However, a substantial portion of the rest of the ancient world is touched upon in the last half of the book of **VII. NT Archae-** Acts, which describes **ology Out-** Paul's missionary jour- **side of** neys. It is therefore of **Palestine** great interest to the Bible student to ascertain the location of these cities, to learn something of their life and culture, and to find whatever light can be thrown upon specific statements about them in the book of the Acts or in any of the Epistles.

The situation of NT archaeology is vastly different from that of OT archaeology. Most of the history of the nations that faced Israel in OT times was completely unknown before the rise of archaeology, but quite a number of books written on papyrus in the Roman Empire in the first century A.D. have been copied and thus preserved. Consequently, the greater part of our information about the background of the latter part of Acts comes not from archaeological discoveries but from manuscripts that have been passed on through the ages. This material is of great importance for the understanding of the Book of the Acts, but does not really come under the head of Biblical archaeology. Discussion of it will be found in the articles in this encyclopedia about the various cities involved.

Considerable archaeological work has been carried on in just about every city named in Acts. While a few of these have continued to be important places through the centuries, some are today comparatively deserted. In the case of a few, the very location was forgotten, but all of these have now been located.

During the closing years of the 19th century, a brilliant English scholar, Sir William Ramsay, undertook to study the ancient geography of Asia Minor. Ramsay had been taught that the Book of the Acts was a forgery of the late second century, untrustworthy in its picture of the early church and empire. He thought it would be interesting to prove from actual observations on the field that the author of the book had fantastically misconstrued the geographical and historical situation that he professed to describe. To Ramsay's amazement, he soon began to find evidence that the statements in Acts reflected accurately the precise situation in the middle of the first century A.D. Ramsay made extensive explorations and investigations and wrote numerous books in support of his altered viewpoint, the exact opposite of that with which he began.

The history and geography of the first century A.D. is a very large subject.

In some of its sections our knowledge is extremely limited, but in others we know a great deal. Comparatively little of this extensive material is involved in the background of the events recorded in the Bible.

B. General Corroboration

The account of Paul's journeys takes for granted a situation in which a very large area of Europe and of Asia is under one political control, so that travel is comparatively unrestricted. A few languages are widely spoken so that communication presents little difficulty. Law and order are quite well maintained. There are groups of Jews in many places, and synagogues are often found. The Roman power is supreme and Roman authority is everywhere recognized. This general situation is amply proven from ancient writings and is further substantiated by archaeological materials.

C. Special Corroboration

Archaeology has provided striking special corroboration of a number of points in the account of Paul's journeys. At that time the governmental situation was exceedingly complex. The Roman conquest had been made in various stages, extending over a long period of time. As a result, the conquered areas, though all under the actual control of the emperor, used a great variety of terms as titles of officials and had many differences as to customs and precise details of administration. Some of these details are well known to us from historical records, others hardly at all. Many passages in the Acts describe Paul's encounter with the political authorities in different cities. It is impressive to note the accuracy with which Luke threads his way through the different governmental districts and the correctness with which he gives the titles, and occasionally the names of the various officials. One especially interesting case relates to Thessalonica. In Acts 17:6 it is stated that Paul's friends were dragged before the rulers of Thessalonica. The Greek form of the word there translated "rulers" is *politarchas*. This particular word occurs nowhere else in any manuscript that has survived from ancient times. Yet within the last century a number of inscriptions have been discovered which give the rulers of Thessalonica this title of politarch, providing a most striking instance of special corroboration of the accuracy of Luke's account.

In the account of Paul's stay in Corinth in Acts 18:12, these words occur: "And when Gallio was the proconsul (AV, "deputy") of Achaia." An inscription has been found on the opposite side of the Gulf of Corinth, six miles inland, which refers to "Lucius Julius Gallio . . . the proconsul of Achaia."

Acts 13:7 names Sergius Paulus as proconsul (AV, "deputy") when Paul visited Cyprus. An inscription of the year A.D. 55 has been found which contains the words, "in the time of the proconsul Paulus." Acts 9:11 relates that a disciple in Damascus was told to go "into the street which is called Straight." A street there still preserves that name. In I Cor. 10:25 Paul says to the people of Corinth: "Whatsoever is sold in the shambles, that eat, asking no question for conscience' sake." The Greek word translated "shambles" (which might also be translated "market") has been found in the remains of ancient Corinth on a store for the selling of meat and other foodstuffs.

Acts 19:23-41 describes a great riot that occurred in Ephesus when the silversmiths feared that Paul's preaching would interfere with their profits from the sale of things related to the worship of Diana. Multitudes gathered in the theater and yelled for two hours: "Great is Diana of the Ephesians." Ancient writings speak of the famous temple of Diana at Ephesus, but it fell into ruins, and one hundred years ago even its location was unknown. In 1863 an English architect, J. T. Wood, went to the ruins of Ephesus in order to find the famous temple, but had to search six years before he succeeded. After much hunting he came upon an inscription which gave a clue to the fact that it was more than one mile NE of the city, and here he found its sculptured columns and massive blocks of marble, 20 feet below the present level of the ground. Later excavations were carried on for many years by the Austrian Archaeological Institute. The temple was found to have been very large and splendidly decorated and many interesting inscriptions were found, corroborating the references in Acts to the worship of Diana at Ephesus.

These are a few examples of the type of special corroboration that is apt to emerge from the discovery of inscriptions and the examination of buildings in the cities visited by Paul. Much more material of the same sort has come to light from the study of the writings that have been handed down by copying and recopying, as shown in the articles on the various cities.

At this point we might also mention some material found outside of Palestine that corroborates certain details of the gospel story. In Egypt papyri have been found referring to the taking of a Roman census every 14 years. Actual census returns have been found, using the same Greek word that Luke 2:2 employs for the enrollment. In addition, evidence from the papyri found in Egypt also corroborates the practice of going to one's own home place for enrollment, as in Luke 2:1-5.

D. Interpretation

The more we know about the life, customs, and geographical situation of the various cities mentioned in the book of Acts or in the NT Epistles, the easier it is to understand the precise meaning of some of the statements made, and the more vividly the situation can be established in our minds. A great deal of material of importance for this purpose is contained in the writings of the geographers Strabo and Pausanias, and a certain amount in the works of Tacitus, Suetonius, and Dio Cassius, although these historians are most interested in the actions of the great emperors, comparatively few of which have any connection with the Bible. A century or two later, when Christianity had become a greater factor, works of general history paid more attention to it.

Archaeological material sometimes contributes to interpretation, as in some of the instances discussed above under Special Corroboration.

E. Derivation

Toward the end of the past century many books were written to show that the distinctive ideas of Christianity were taken over from various heathen religions. Similar ideas are widely taught today. It is alleged that during the first century A.D. various mystery cults and pagan religions made their way from the E into many sections of the Roman Empire, and that Christianity was merely the particular one of these movements that happened to win out.

Discussion of this idea of deriving Christianity from pagan sources involves evidence of various types. At this point we shall restrict ourselves to noting two ways in which archaeological research affects the discussion.

The first of these relates to the Dead Sea Scrolls. Though greatly used as evidence for a claim of derivation of Christianity from Jewish sources (see discussion in VI.F. above), the Scrolls strike a blow against the claim of derivation from heathen sources. Many Christian ideas or terms that are said to be derived from heathen religions have been found in expressions in the Dead Sea Scrolls. This does not mean to say that these ideas were derived by Christianity from this Jewish sect. However, it does show that many ideas that have been alleged to show pagan influence were actually common in the Jewish culture at the very time of the rise of Christianity.

In the second place, we note the relation of archaeological evidence to the widespread claim that pagan religions and mystery sects were struggling to fill a vacuum in the Roman Empire during the first century. During the first half of the present century, extensive excavations were carried out in Egypt, Syria, Palestine, and other regions. These excavations have brought to light many evidences of the well-established pagan religions, of the presence of Jewish groups, and of early Christian developments, but practically nothing in the way of other types of religious writings or religious structures from this early period. The mystery religions and Gnostic groups that struggled against Christianity in the second and third centuries A.D. are scarcely evidenced at all for the first century. Some of these rose as an attempt to combat the rising power of Christianity; many of them show borrowing from Christianity; most of them were not even in existence when Christianity began. Thus archaeological evidence helps to show that the rise of Christianity is a unique historical phenomenon, and not simply one of many competing mystery cults filling a vacuum in the Roman Empire.

F. Conclusion Regarding Biblical Archaeology

At the end of section V a brief conclusion regarding OT archaeology was given. We have noticed that NT archaeology is different in some regards. Yet it involves the same four general areas of interest. Archaeology has produced many bits of interesting confirmatory evidence as to the accuracy and dependability of both the Old and New Testaments. Nothing has been discovered in archaeology that would show fraud, misrepresentation, or error in either Testament. We cannot expect to prove the Bible by archaeology. The great subjects with which the Bible primarily deals — man's relation to God, and God's provision for man's salvation—are matters that are not susceptible to archaeological evidence. However, archaeology demolishes many of the attacks that unbelievers have made against the Bible, and it disproves many of the arguments advanced to show that Christianity is merely the result of a historical development. In addition, archaeological material gives help for the precise understanding of many Biblical statements.

BIBLIOGRAPHY:

W. F. Albright, *The Archaeology of Palestine* (1949; latest ed. 1960).

W. F. Albright, *From the Stone Age to Christianity* (Baltimore, 1940; 2nd ed. 1957).

G. A. Barton, *Archaeology and the Bible* (Philadelphia, 1916; 7th ed. 1937).

M. Burrows, *The Dead Sea Scrolls* (New York, 1955).

M. Burrows, *More About the Dead Sea Scrolls* (New York, 1958).

S. L. Caiger, *Archaeology of the New Testament* (London, 1939; 2nd ed. 1948).

A. Erman and H. Ranke, *Aegypten und Aegyptisches Leben im Altertum* (Tubingen, 1923).

A. Erman, *The Literature of the Ancient Egyptians*, tr. into Eng. by A. M. Blackman (London, 1927).

J. Finegan, *Light from the Ancient Past* (Princeton, 1946; 2nd ed. 1959).

J. P. Free, *Archaeology and Bible History* (Wheaton, 1950).

M. G. Kyle, *Excavating Kirjath-sepher's Ten Cities* (Grand Rapids, 1934).

C. Marston, *The Bible Comes Alive* (London, 1937; 5th ed. 1940), 111-250.

J. B. Pritchard, *The Ancient Near East, an Anthology of Texts and Pictures* (Princeton, 1958).

J. B. Pritchard, *Ancient Near Eastern Pictures Relating to the Old Testament* (Princeton, 1954).

J. B. Pritchard, ed., *Ancient Near Eastern Texts Relating to the Old Testament* (Princeton, 1950; 2nd ed. 1955).

S. J. Schultz, *The Old Testament Speaks* (New York, 1960).

D. W. Thomas, ed., *Documents from Old Testament Times* (New York, 1961).

M. F. Unger, *Archaeology and the New Testament* (Grand Rapids, 1962).

M. F. Unger, *Archaeology and the Old Testament* (Grand Rapids, 1954).

G. E. Wright, *Biblical Archaeology*, il. rev. ed. (Philadelphia, 1963).

ALLAN A. MACRAE

About the Author

ALLAN A. MacRAE, A.B.,A.M., Th.B., Ph.D., is President and Professor of Old Testament at Faith Theological Seminary, located at 920 Spring Avenue, Elkins Park, Pennsylvania.

Dr. MacRae's learned and extensive knowledge in both the Biblical and archaeological fields has been acquired through many years of exhaustive study and research together with over thirty years of theological seminary teaching.

Dr. MacRae received his academic training at Occidental College, A.B., 1922; ibid., A.M., 1923; Princeton Theological Seminary, Th.B., 1927; Princeton University, A.M., 1927; University of Berlin, 1927-29; American School of Oriental Research, 1929; and, University of Pennsylvania, Ph.D., 1936.